METALLICA
KILL'EM ALL
THEIR GREATEST LIVE PERFORMANCES

Marc Aumont

greenfinch

Sitting down to write a book about the legend that is Metallica, covering countless tours and thousands of concerts, was a dizzying task. It soon became clear that we couldn't include everything. Churning out a running commentary of each show from A to Z also seemed pointless; the book would be far too long and repetitive. As well as there not being enough reliable source material, going over and over the weary routine of tour life would quickly become dull and irrelevant.

While every single one of the band's concerts is important in its own way, many shows stand out for individual reasons. Some are important milestones: the band's first-ever gig, the first American tour, or the first tour around Europe, during which the band forged a special bond with the continent. Legendary stadium performances and emblematic festivals came later, and audiences became more and more mainstream. There is a pattern to this book, but it is subjective. It focuses on Metallica's anthology concerts and tours. The highs, the lows, the dramas and extravagances, the thrills, spills, joys and challenges. The ups and downs of life on the road that tell a fascinating story, a modern-day odyssey.

We're obviously taking a risk by concentrating on a selection of standout shows and tours. Indeed, some diehard fans might be disappointed that their favourite performance has been left out. Seeing Metallica in action is such an incredible experience that everyone in the audience leaves with a special memory of their own, especially devoted fans. By not including every gig, we run the risk of ignoring a show that had an impact on a reader obsessed with *Ride the Lightning* or angering another who thinks that the band wrote nothing of note after *Master of Puppets*. We hear you. This book has been fuelled by a lasting love for the band that runs deep. A sincere passion that we hope you will share as you read it. Strap yourself in and enjoy the ride.

CONTENTS

INTRODUCTION

You are about to read a story that many aspiring musicians would describe as a dream come true: the Holy Grail. A group of young men get together to make music (in a newly coined genre called thrash) and end up forging a friendship that leads them to the heights of stardom. Lars and James met in April 1981, but their first encounter was a let-down to say the least. James, a guitar player, and Ron McGovney who plays bass, have just started auditioning drummers to join their band. Hugh Tanner had introduced the two musicians, convincing Lars to try his luck, but James and Ron were unimpressed with Lars and his lacklustre audition. 'When he [James] and Lars first jammed, I thought Lars was the worst drummer I had ever heard in my life! He couldn't keep a beat, and compared to Mulligan, he just couldn't play. So I told James, "This guy sucks, dude."' James also remembers the audition. 'Lars had a pretty crappy drum kit, with one cymbal. It kept falling over, and we'd have to stop, and he'd pick the fucking thing up. He really was not a good drummer... When we were done jamming, it was, what the fuck was that? We stiffed him on the bill for the studio, too.'

Despite the setback, Lars got back in touch a year later, hoping to convince James to give him a second chance. He wanted them to record a track for Brian Slagel, the CEO of Metal Blade, who was getting ready to release an anthology called *The New Heavy Metal Revue Presents Metal Massacre*. James agreed and set up a second audition at Ron's house. The guitarist was instantly struck by how much progress young Lars had made since they first met.

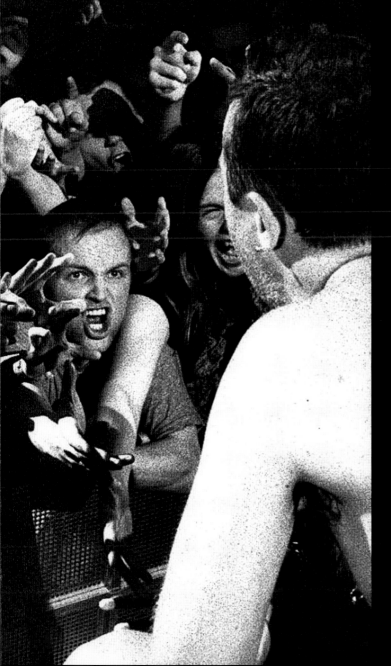

'Lars had improved as a drummer a whole lot. He also had a brand-new drum kit, a genuine Camco.' The two musicians finally saw eye to eye. Their friendship blossoms through their shared passion for music, conversation and finding new talent, and they began working together. "Hit the Lights", Metallica's first proper track, was released in the same year as Slagel's compilation album, *Metal Massacre*. Metallica was born and a long and thrilling journey had begun.

Many still call this band the greatest of all time. Legends. The kings of metal. When Lars and James decided to form the band (a proto-Metallica if you like), neither of them could imagine that they – among millions of other aspiring young musicians – would go on to revolutionize music and change their own destinies forever.

Why has Metallica been so successful? First, timing. The band was formed right when thrash was on the rise, and the foursome did much of the legwork to get this innovative subgenre of heavy metal off the ground. Their outstanding creative talent can't be overlooked either: who could forget the solid steel riff in "Master of Puppets" or the chiselled power of "Nothing Else Matters"? But the biggest draw for Metallica's legions of fans is most certainly their showmanship.

For most aspiring stars, their first gigs are in small clubs and things are difficult and messy. With Metallica though, something truly magical happens when they go wild on stage. Though they hadn't yet been nicknamed The Four Horsemen, the energy they brought to the new thrash scene took them all around the United States. They do nothing by halves. Dizzy with the euphoria of touring, with its endless bus trips and overheated dressing rooms, the band members throw themselves into their new lives in the big leagues.

When the first European dates began rolling in, the band realize that they have become too big to stay on home turf . Years later, all their tours are shared between the United States and Europe. The band plans gigs and festivals all around the world (South America, the Pacific, Asia) and their shows grow bigger and better.

But their phenomenal success was no easy ride. Along the way, there are deaths, physical and mental injuries, inevitable evictions and tension. The musicians grow up as Metallica matures, just like their early fans. The diehards are always in the front row at their concerts, even 40 years later. Crammed in against the crash barriers, they lift their arms high as soon as they hear the first notes of Ennio Morricone's *The Ecstasy of Gold*, which the band uses as an introduction for most of their concerts.

It's a symbol of the power that live music can wield over the people who play it, and those who listen. Metallica have been performing on stages around the world almost non-stop since the very beginning. The faces of the musicians now bear the scars of their hectic life on the road. The element of surprise has faded, and the unbridled debauchery of the early days has given way to greater musical mastery. But the magic lives on, and seeing Metallica on stage is an experience nobody can forget. As you leaf through the pages of this book, we invite you to explore the making of a miracle, to look back at the main events and concerts that forged the stage careers of James, Lars, Kirk and all the others. We open the door to the tour bus and take you inside, we lift the curtain on dressing-room rehearsals and sleepless nights in hotel rooms. Come with us and relive the glory days of what is still – 50 years on – the greatest metal band of all time.

Previous page: Excerpt from Some Kind of Monster *(2004) by Joe Berlinger and Bruce Sinofsky, which follows the thrash metal legends as they work on the* St. Anger *album. Opposite: James Hetfield's first performance at Ruthie's Inn in Berkeley, California on 24 August 1985.*

TRIAL BY FIRE

Metallica was now considered one of the greatest metal bands of all time, playing to packed stadiums and headlining the world's biggest heavy metal music festivals. But the early days were quite different for the foursome.

A shaky line-up, stage fright, musical mishaps, concert flops and empty venues: the future Four Horsemen experienced no shortage of setbacks when they began performing. And as real success glimmered on the horizon in late summer 1982 and the band agreed to more and more concert dates, Metallica were no different to other metal bands, quickly consumed by the tribulations of harsh tour life, with its share of ego battles and alcohol abuse.

Their early days were certainly rough, but things began to settle at the start of 1983 when the band recorded its first two albums, *Kill'Em All* and *Ride the Lightning*.

A BAPTISM OF FIRE

With their line-up still finding its feet, Metallica took to the stage for the first time in 1982. Though their enthusiasm took the band to a certain point, they failed to win over large audiences. Stories from these first performances given by the greatest thrash band in history paint a picture of their early days.

AT RADIO CITY: THE FIRST LIVE SHOW
Anaheim, California · 14 March 1982

After weeks of rigorous rehearsing, Metallica got its first gig. Booked to appear at Radio City Music Hall, the band was determined to make a lasting impression. The bill for the concert made no bones about their lofty ambition: "Metallica (Metalus Maximus)".

The band led by James Hetfield only on vocals, with Dave Mustaine covering the guitar parts, took to the stage... and played a set of covers! The fledgling band's repertoire was a little thin, but they had no qualms lifting tracks by New Wave of British Heavy Metal (NWOBHM) bands without mentioning it to the audience!

A legend was born, but the evening itself was a damp squib. As with most first concerts, the boys had to deal with technical issues as well as their obvious lack of experience, shyness and mismanaged anger. Dave couldn't get his distortion pedal to work and broke a string right at the start of "Hit the Lights"! Unfortunately, as the only guitarist in a thrash band, the "Metallica sound" depends on him.

Everything went quiet and James had no idea how to fill the void. Dave knelt and restrung his instrument in an awkward silence. Despite this lacklustre performance peppered with disasters, Metallica managed to find its mojo. John Kornarens, friend of the band and future journalist, who was at that concert, remembers: 'I liked the music, it had a real European edge to it. It was heavy and it was street, it had a lot of energy to it and it was very aggressive.'

Previous page: The first concert in the Netherlands at the Aardschok festival in Isselhal (Zwolle), 11 February 1984. Opposite: Lars Ulrich and James Hetfield at the Aardschok festival on the same day.

METALLICA
(METALUS MAXIMUS)

THE YOUNG METAL ATTACK

Hit the Lights
Blitzkrieg
Helpless
Jump in the Fire
Let It Loose
Sucking My Love
Am I Evil?
The Prince
Killing Time

THE FUTURE RIFFING MACHINE

'God will make everything right.' That's what James Hetfield was brought up to believe. He was born in California on 3 August 1963. His father was a truck driver and his mother a singer. Their religious beliefs shaped his childhood and had a strong influence on most of his teenage years and adult life. His parents, Virgil and Cynthia, were active in the Christian Science community, and his father even taught Sunday School classes.

James had an outstanding aptitude for music at a very early age, and his parents decided to sign him up for piano lessons. He kept up his playing for two years. His older brother played the drums, and when young James tried out his kit, something magical happened. He had a great sense of rhythm and turned out to be an excellent musician. He took up the guitar during his teenage years.

His parents' divorce in 1976 left James deeply affected. He formed his very first band in 1980 and called it Obsession. His second band, Syrinx, came next, but disaster struck once more: his mother passed away from cancer, which she had left untreated for religious reasons. James was bereft and went on to express his feelings of loss later in his career, with "The God That Failed" and "Mama Said".

But for now, James was just 16 years old. He moved to Brea and started at a new high school. He set up Phantom Lord, which later became Leather Charm. Not yet a metalhead, his musical style was full-on glam rock! Around the same time, he went to see Aerosmith in concert at the California World Music Festival, and his life changed forever. The attitude of the musicians and Steven Tyler's showmanship in front of the crowd inspired him to work harder to achieve his musical ambitions.

Separation and death had haunted his teenage years and had left James with an itch to scratch. He wanted to push himself beyond his limit. This love for excess was revealed a few years later when he started hanging out at parties with other musicians, drinking and partying hard.

James found that Metallica gave him the perfect opportunity to indulge in the vices of rock'n'roll during that pivotal time of late adolescence.

WHISKY A GO GO: THE SPRINGBOARD?

West Hollywood, California
27 March 1982

As we have seen, the young band's first show was a letdown. But Metallica didn't give up. The musicians managed to secure a new date and destiny stepped in. Ron McGovney, who at that time was a photographer for the infamous Mötley Crüe, heard through the grapevine that a gig was planned for the band on 27 March at the legendary Whisky A Go Go club. They were billed to support Saxon, an NWOBHM heavyweight.

The bassist persuaded Metallica to record a three-track demo of "Hit the Lights", "Killing Time" and "Let It Loose" as soon as possible. His plan was to get the tape to the club's owners and convince them to book Metallica as the opening act for this metal extravaganza. While Ron was waiting at the entrance to the club, cassette tape in hand, he bumped into Mötley Crüe. The band gave Metallica a chance to replace them as Saxon's opening act. Mötley Crüe claimed that they were 'too famous for that now!' This tremendous stroke of luck put Metallica on stage at the legendary club on 27 March 1982, opening for one of the most famous metal bands of the time.

Even though covers account for almost half the set, Metallica managed to fit in some of their best originals, including a new song written by Mustaine, "Metal Militia", based on an assault-tank riff in the purest thrash tradition, mixing raw energy and the melodies that make his guitar playing so distinctive. Legend has it that the band also bought a few accessories to wear at their first few concerts: the musicians are said to have passed around a bandolier with a skull on it for them each to wear.

But despite their immense determination and nerves of steel, the thrash musicians didn't quite win over the audience.

Gene
HOGLAN

'They weren't very good. They were sloppy and kind of ugly. Poor James, it was only his second show or something, but I remember him kind of crawling behind the amps and letting Mustaine do all the talking.'

John
BUSH

'James was just singing, no guitar, and wearing leopard-skin pants. They were not very good!'

The legendary Whisky A Go Go

Opening on 15 January 1964, the club took its name from the first-ever nightclub created in Paris in 1947. As its customers were mainly American sailors, they brought the concept back to the United States in the 1950s. The West Hollywood club broke the law from the very first day it opened. It was prohibited from hosting live music events but organized a Johnny Rivers concert.

The "Whisky" earned itself a reputation for breaking the rules, and the police marched The Doors off the stage in 1966, right in the middle of their famous track, "The End". The club was also the scene of the Sunset Strip riots that same year. In the early 80s, everyone in the US heavy metal and punk scene was desperate to play at the venue and it became a legendary melting pot for every style of alternative music.

THE CONCERT FACTORY...
Costa Mesa, California · 23 April 1982

Despite two rather average performances, April saw Metallica taking a shot at a gig in Costa Mesa's Concert Factory. They had learned some lessons from the first two shows and had decided to bring on a second guitarist to strengthen their line-up. That's when Brad Parker was chosen to join the ranks.

But while the band was waiting in the dressing rooms before going on stage, something rather unusual happened. Ron remembers 'hearing a guitar solo'. He goes on: 'So we look over the railing of the dressing room, and we see Brad onstage just blazing away on his guitar. So that was Metallica's first and last gig with Brad.' The guitarist had apparently decided to show off his solo skills before Metallica came on stage! The aggressive move tipped the testy Dave Mustaine over the edge, and the other young band members joined him!

That evening Metallica added a new track to its repertoire, "The Mechanix", with its powerful riff designed to smash up the asphalt like a horde of wild bikers. The song also appeared on the list for the next demo, alongside "Hit the Lights", "Jump in the Fire" and "Motorbreath", another unreleased track.

...AND BACK BAY HIGH SCHOOL
Costa Mesa, California · 25 May 1982

Metallica played another gig on 25 May 1985 in an odd venue – Lars's former high school. The set list was now much more extensive because it included ten tracks, five of which were originals. Unfortunately, the high school audience members were quite different from the Whisky A Go Go regulars, and the room gradually emptied during the show, leaving the band practically alone. The seemingly disastrous event stood out for one reason, though: for the first time ever, James sang AND played the rhythm guitar.

This was a pivotal moment in the band's history because the musician would never again appear without his favourite instrument. Despite tension running high between the band members (especially Dave Mustaine and Ron, the bassist), the band continued on the gig circuit throughout the summer of 1982.

A DRUMMER WITH AMBITION

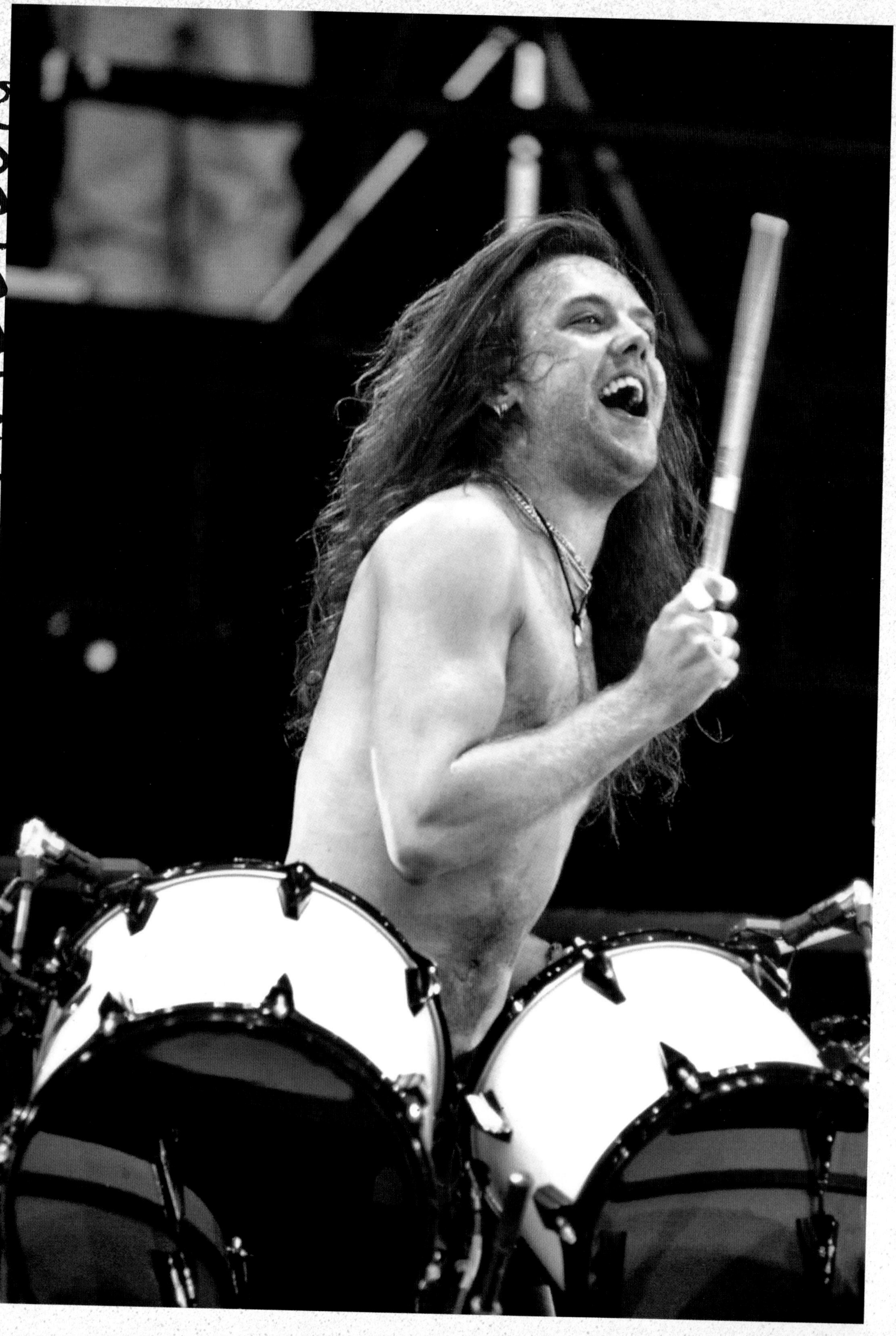

Hated by some, mocked by others, often considered arrogant, Lars is a force of nature in metal music. He was born on 26 December 1963 in Gentofte, Denmark. His father, Torben, was a renowned tennis player, as well as an actor, musician, writer and painter.

Something happened to him as a young boy that would one day drive Lars to perform on stages around the world. He was ten years old when his father took him to Rome to see a concert by his saxophonist friend, Dexter Gordon. During the show, young Lars climbed on stage, grabbed the microphone, sang and ran around for a few minutes. A star was born. Admittedly, Lars's father, a real jack-of-all-trades with a passion for culture, had already encouraged his young son to take a keen interest in cinema, jazz and philosophy, and musicians visited their family home regularly. A year earlier, when the boy was just nine years old, family friend and jazzman Ray Moore took him to his very first gig. It was a revelation for Lars and after the show, he rushed to buy the band's album. The record was *Fireball*, and the band was the now legendary Deep Purple. This was Lars's first encounter with rock, and a never-ending love affair began.

In 1980, the Ulrich family decided to leave Copenhagen and settle in Newport Beach, a small town on the outskirts of Los Angeles. At the time, Lars followed in his father's footsteps and set his sights on a career in tennis. Despite his aptitude for the sport, the "Deep Purple effect" took hold of Lars and he was torn between two paths. Torben was open-minded and decided not to force his son into a specific career. He let destiny take control. In 1977, his parents gave him his very first drum kit, and Lars spent many hours in his room repeatedly playing Deep Purple (obviously) and Kiss records. Around the same time, the future drummer showed an interest in heavy metal, much to his father's amusement. He scoured record shops, collected records, met Brian Slagel, and decided on an ambition: one day he would have his own heavy metal band.

KEYSTONE: THE FIRST REAL SUCCESS
San Francisco, California
18 September 1982

A twist of fate gave Metallica a chance to do their first show in San Francisco. Brian Slagel – who had released the *Metal Massacre* compilation a few months prior, which featured Metallica's "Hit the Lights" – was organizing a PR event to celebrate the release of the seminal record. The line-up for the show included several bands he had signed for the compilation, including one that is now forgotten: Cirith Ungol.

A few days before this famous "Metal Massacre Night", Cirith Ungol withdrew, leaving a spot available between Hans Naughty and Bitch, two other bands. The manager called Metallica. The opportunity was too good to pass up and the band took up the challenge on 18 September at Keystone. Confident in their ability, the boys threw themselves into a set of seven tracks from the *No Life* demo and performed two covers by Diamond Head. The audience was putty in the hands of this new metal band. The band were the first to be surprised when they realized that the demo they had recorded in LA had made its way to California through the magic of tape trading! The fans were hysterical and some of the audience swarmed onto the stage in the middle of the concert in a frenzy of wild headbanging. At the end of the show, Ron still couldn't believe that this audience knew their song lyrics by heart, let alone how crazed some people were to get close to James and his band in search of autographs.

The Metallica machine was set in motion. The members noticed that crowds in San Francisco were much more receptive to their music than those in Los Angeles, where glam and hair metal still reigned supreme, and they realized that San Francisco was about to become Metallica's Mecca.

Jeff
BECERRA

'I remember seeing Metallica at the Keystone Berkeley and thinking, wow – these guys are tremendous.'

Ron
McGOVNEY

'I was kind of their babysitter, you might say. They would get stinking drunk all the time but I was the person who was elected to drive them everywhere. [...] I was the road manager and had to book the hotels, drive the trailer, load the equipment, while they sat in the back of the van and drank a gallon of vodka and got totally ripped and said, "Ron's such a jerk, blah blah blah." They came to hate me... it came to the point where they couldn't stand me any more and I couldn't stand them any more, and they started looking for another bass player.'

The roads of hell

Things really took off for the band in the late summer of 1982 and the autumn that followed. But this year was tough first because of the band's fragile line-up, and second because the musicians found out what life on the road was really like, with its adventures, overindulgence, and the inevitable tension that goes with living in each other's pockets.

They drank too much and the exhausting journeys between each concert only heightened tensions among the band. A humiliated Ron McGovney was close to breaking point. Dave Mustaine was gradually becoming an alcoholic, which didn't help his erratic behaviour and character.

To make matters worse, Lars and James also fell into a drinking frenzy...

It was time to turn the page on this early rocky period for the young band, whose exasperated bassist soon left. Enter Cliff Burton, and the real beginning of the band's entry into the heavy metal history books.

THE CHILDHOOD FRIEND

'Everybody had their little clique... there were the cheerleaders, the jocks, the marching band people... and you ended up with the laggers hanging around without any real social group, and that included James and I'.

That is how Ron McGovney describes his first memories with James. Born on 2 November 1962, he met the future guitarist and star of Metallica at Downey High School, south of Los Angeles. They discovered rock'n'roll together, and fought over who they thought was the best band: Kiss or Aerosmith.

In 1980 Hetfield started a band called Obsession, and naturally Ron joined as the bass player. When proto-Metallica began to take shape, the first rehearsals were arranged at Ron's house. But Mustaine's bad jokes and the inces-sant taunts of the excited young men on tour quickly got the better of his childhood friend, who threw in the towel before Metallica could enjoy its first real success.

Ron left the band just before it shot to stardom, and never really came back to music. He reappeared alongside his ex-bandmates in 2011 when he was invited to celebrate Metallica's 30th anniversary. Eight years later, in 2019, he published a photo of himself on X (previously Twitter) with Lars, James, Kirk and Robert Trujillo, taken on the day of this final reunion and commented: 'My 1982 Wash-burn B-20 bass and I posing with the @Metallica boys in 2011. I don't know when I have felt more out of place in my life.' His post says it all.

FROM SAN FRANCISCO TO NEW YORK

At the end of 1982, the band packed up and moved to San Francisco, which was the deal-breaking condition that the coveted bassist Cliff Burton set before agreeing to join the band. A few weeks after Ron McGovney left, Cliff joined Lars and James for their first rehearsal. It was 28 December 1982 and Metallica's soon-to-be legendary line-up was finally complete...

THE STONE: A RENAISSANCE BEGINS
San Francisco, California · 5 March 1983

Having just arrived in San Francisco, the band moved into the El Cerrito neighbourhood and began doing what they do best: partying and making music. The new Metallica started practising together and Cliff brought something special to the sound. The quartet was rejuvenated and confident when they showed up to play at The Stone, the high chapel of the San Francisco metal scene, on 5 March 1983. The band had more experience at this point, but for the audience, and indeed the other members of Metallica, the evening would forever remain the "Cliff Burton revelation". Dressed in bell-bottom jeans and with a slightly old-fashioned hippie look, his bushy hair blowing around his face, Metallica's new bassist was a breath of fresh air compared with the cartridge belts and bare torsos of the other musicians. But it was his musical performance that really stood out.

While the band finished its sequence of well-known tracks ("Hit the Lights", "The Mechanix" and so on) and new releases ("No Remorse" with its turbo-armoured finale), Cliff finally played a bass solo lasting almost five minutes that he wrote himself, entitled "(Anesthesia) Pulling Teeth". Struck chords and classical motifs flowed into each other seamlessly, and the audience was mesmerized by the extraordinary virtuoso bass player whose fingers moved across the fretboard at warp speed. This show was an opportunity for the new musician to make his mark. His melodic, aggressive, uptempo playing and characteristic sound were created by the perfect balance he stuck between his finger-playing groove and the snapping distortion of string against fret. The audience was thirsty for more, going wild when the band picked the tempo back up with "Whiplash", at the time the fastest song in its repertoire. Then came "Am I Evil?" "The Prince", "Blitzkrieg", and the final blow came to the white-hot crowd when the band charge into "Metal Militia".

San Francisco, the homeland of thrash

It was no coincidence that the members of Metallica decided one fine morning to fill a truck and head off to the Californian capital. At the time, the Los Angeles scene was dominated by hair metal bands, and Metallica's thrash was struggling to get a foothold with audiences who were more accustomed to permed hair than fierce saturation on double bass drums. For the band's new fanbase, San Francisco was the place to be for new metal: more specific media, more open-mindedness to new musical trends and more legendary clubs already plugging into the thrash channel, like Ruthie's, Waldorf and The Stone, the famous venue where Metallica played its first gig in the city.

San Francisco certainly had the clubs, but another reason for them coming was that professionals like Brian Slagel and his label were also here, feeding a horde of young fans eager for a new sound like the one Lars and his bandmates were making. The legendary Californian bay soon becomes home to what would be known as "Bay Area Thrash". The expression refers to a genre that originated in Europe and was transformed by myriad bands that are still active and famous today: Exodus, Possessed and... Metallica.

THE UNPREDICTABLE...

Dave was born sometime around midnight on 13 September 1961 and had a turbulent childhood that affected him for many years.

He was born in La Mesa, California, to alcoholic parents. His father was violent and regularly mistreated his mother, Emily. Dave and his mother never settled anywhere for long, moving around California from place to place in a bid to escape the domestic violence.

In 1974, Dave discovered pop through his sister, a fan of Cat Stevens. Soon fed up with the mournful musical style, he turned to rock and became a fan of Led Zeppelin, drawn like many other teens to the band's electric energy. As a teenager, he was fascinated by martial arts and the occult, and began learning the guitar. He joined a band called Panic and amassed an impressive collection of amps and guitars. He was eventually scouted by Metallica, who were on the lookout for a second guitarist. The band briefly auditioned him and told him that he had the job, even though he'd barely finished tuning his instrument.

Unpredictable on stage and quickly struggling with severe alcohol issues, Dave was a brawler with natural confidence who, from the first performances with Metallica, did whatever he could to upstage James, who at the time was less self-confident. The rest is history.

HELLO NEW YORK, GOODBYE MUSTAINE
March 1983–April 1984

Metallica's melodic, fast and aggressive style of music started making waves all over the country through tape trading. One of the band's cassettes landed in the hands of Jon Zazula, a concert organizer, band manager and owner of a New York record store. He was immediately struck by what he describes as a fusion between Motörhead and NWOBHM, but with an American feel. He picked up the phone and asked Metallica to get straight to NYC. The meeting came at the perfect time: the band members had just decided that it was high time they took their music nationwide.

At the end of March 1983, Metallica rented two vans, loaded all their belongings inside and headed off to the Big Apple, 2,500 miles away. During the long journey, Dave's erratic behaviour revealed a rather worrying side of his personality. 'We'd never been out of California, and we got there to find out we were having some real problems with Dave's attitude. He couldn't really handle being away from home or something... we knew it couldn't go on like that, so we started looking at other stuff.'

The band played two concerts in New York on 8 and 9 April, opening for Vandenberg and The Rods at the Paramount Theater and at L'Amour in Brooklyn. The two concerts went without a hitch, but the band and its managers had already come to a decision. On Sunday 10 April, Metallica took a day off, planning to make their move on Monday morning.

Legend has it that when he woke up, Mustaine found that his bags had been packed. The other members of the band were standing around him, stone-faced. They told him he was no longer part of Metallica and that a bus was coming to pick him up in an hour. On 11 April 1983, Dave travelled back to San Francisco. He only rejoined the band as second guitarist on rare occasions, for specific events, many years later.

Lars
ULRICH

'On the big continental trip from San Francisco to New York it all kind of spilled over – there were a few things happening that became too much. The guy couldn't control himself under various situations. On a long-term basis, it would have become a problem.'

Before the internet: tape trading

If you wanted to get your music known outside your circle of influence during the 80s, tape trading was the only way to do it. A band would record a demo or a live performance and hand out cassette copies through networks of agents, record stores, fans, independent label bosses and club owners.

The tapes would be sent out by post, hundreds of them weaving an invisible web among members of the same community, flowing all over the United States and around Europe.

One of Metallica's cassettes ended up on the desk of Zazula, the boss of a record store in New York, who convinced the band to come to the Big Apple...

KILL'EM ALL FOR ONE: THE FIRST BIG TOUR

Metallica began 1983 in an unfamiliar city, far from home. The band had been on an incredible journey before finally launching its first album, *Kill'Em All*. The stage set-up at last met the high standards demanded by Lars and James. For this first record, the band perfectly channelled all the passion, speed, energy and aggressiveness of their music. As soon as the record was released, a two-month tour was planned with British power trio, Raven.

James HETFIELD

'Cliff is the best bass player I've ever worked with. He's a real fuckin' genius. Great guy too, very laid-back. There's a whole different bottom end to the sound now.'

Lars ULRICH

'Kirk plays all the time, he gets up in the morning and just jams. For nine days in the band he's real tight... he's got a lot of good material that we're gonna start using.'

THE SHOWPLACE: KIRK HAMMETT'S FIRST APPEARANCE ON STAGE

Dover, New Jersey · 16 April 1983

When Dave was fired from the band, James and Lars already had an eye on Kirk, a guitarist from another thrash outfit: Exodus. Dissatisfied with his original band, Kirk aced his audition with Metallica in New York and fitted right in. After Hurricane Mustaine, everyone breathed a sigh of relief!

As the opening act for Anthrax, Metallica gave its first performance with Kirk on 16 April 1983, at Showplace, New Jersey. Kirk seemed right at home from the very start and was an exemplary second guitarist. The band's confidence was restored. A good thing too, because Metallica now had the chance to support their British idols, NWOBHM veterans, Venom. This was a masterstroke by Zazula, who had a talent for unearthing bands that were still underground, yet ready for stardom and able to open

for a big name like Venom. With their chaotic concerts, alcohol-fuelled afterparties and endless mayhem, the two bands got along wonderfully and sold out to masses of devoted fans. The tour started with a bang, playing two shows, 22 April and 24 April 1983 at the Paramount Theater on Staten Island. The mood at these high-octane events was captured perfectly in the story of the fire that almost destroyed the hall on 22 April. Venom's roadies, who had apparently overdone it on the flash powder for the pyrotechnic effects, caused a gigantic explosion in the middle of the concert, leaving a four-foot hole in the stage.

Fans loved the on-stage chaos during the concerts, and the two bands let off plenty of steam backstage too. One night, they almost burned down Zazula's kitchen while attempting to cook some food! James Hetfield almost did himself some serious harm when he tripped over holding a bottle of vodka, and one morning, the members of the two bands couldn't believe their eyes when they woke up to find Lars and Cronos in the same bed, dead drunk! When Lars woke up, he started screaming, and was almost knocked out by one of the band's roadies who, clearly, needed a bit more sleep...

Flying V, Marshall wall, white sneakers and leather jacket: Kirk's 80s thrash outfit.

WINNING OVER THE WEST
27 July–3 September 1983

No pain, no gain: that's a perfect way to sum up the state of mind during the tour that brought Metallica in line with Raven. The name of the tour was a combination of the two albums that the bands wanted to promote: *Kill'Em All* for Metallica and *All For One* for Raven. The tour was given the name Kill'Em All For One. Metallica matured during this period of back-to-back concerts. It was an opportunity for the band to build a solid fanbase across most of the United States, and really find its feet on stage. Concert after concert, the band improved musically and on stage. A few years later, James Hetfield admitted that on this tour, Metallica found inspiration in the stage performances of their fellow travellers to ramp up the energy of their shows. Even though the performances were a treat for the crowds, the two bands struggled with conditions backstage. All the musicians slept in a trailer with the roadies and there were no prizes for gues-

sing that with two metal bands living in close quarters, the drinking was heavy, even in the daytime, and the unbearably high temperatures didn't help matters as the tour made its way south. The air conditioning broke down just as they arrived in the scorching heat of Texas. James looks back: 'it was like travelling in an oven. You woke up in the morning, and your tongue was stuck to your palate, because it was 200 degrees in there!'

After this experience, Metallica was determined to move on to the next level. The band produced a show with no expensive staging or decor, and focused on getting closer to the crowd, lapping up its energy, sharing the power of the songs and its aggressive tone. The choice paid dividends, because James came out of the shadows and grew in confidence in his role as frontman. From that point on, he encouraged the crowd to join in during the chorus of the formidable track "Seek & Destroy".

Below: James Hetfield, Cliff Burton and Kirk Hammett at Broadway Jack's in Chicago, 15 December 1983.
Opposite: The Four Horsemen at their best, backstage at Mickey's (Wisconsin) on 13 August 1983.

Party, party, PARTY

As well as upping their performance game, the band members took their partying a notch higher too. The hotels must still bear the scars of the endless drinking fests they indulged in after their electrifying shows. In November 1983, after a few gigs with Armored Saint, Metallica went wild after a particularly heavy drinking binge. A few years later, James remembers it well: 'We went up to Joey's room and drank all his beer. We were all getting really ripped and started throwing bottles out the window. They were smashing and it sounded really neat. But that soon got boring, so I threw Joey's black and red jacket out and it landed in the pool, which luckily had its cover on. So we went down to get it and on the way back up to the tenth floor, we got stuck [...]. We finally get up to the tenth floor and by now I'm pretty mad so I see this fire extinguisher hanging on the wall. So I kinda took it down and started squirting people with it – all this CO2 or some kinda shit was comin' out of it.'

Barely five months after releasing their first album, a long series of gigs, and outrageous behaviour that should have left them feeling satisfied, the musicians of Metallica were already thinking about what came next. Back in New Jersey, the band began writing again for what would be the second album. They performed the new songs at gigs in Cleveland, Chicago and New York with Anthrax, another living legend of thrash.

1984 A PIVOTAL YEAR

The band had given countless sellout concerts in the United States and started the year with a new goal: to create a worthy successor to their celebrated first album. In *Ride the Lightning*, Metallica developed a more polished style and took its creativity even further. The next tour was an opportunity to win over fans in Europe and the four thrash musicians joined forces with their old friends from Venom on an epic adventure.

"FADE TO BLACK": THE CHANNEL CLUB
Boston, Massachusetts · 18 January 1984

Before meeting up with old friends, Metallica gave a series of gigs in the United States at the beginning of January, in New York on the 7th and 11th, then in New Jersey on the 15th. On the 18th, the band went to Boston for an iconic show in the city's legendary venue: Channel. The club closed in 1991, after hosting all the top metal bands of the late 80s. The venue held around 1,700 people, but it had a reputation for going well over that limit. The doors opened at 5 p.m. for the beginning of the show, but the band's equipment had been stolen from the car park. Did someone break into the truck? Did the thieves drive off with the loaded vehicle? Accounts vary, but one thing is certain: James was destroyed when his beloved Marshall amp disappeared. The loss inspired him to write "Fade to Black", on the *Ride the Lightning* album (and the band confirms the story). Obviously, the show couldn't go ahead and a deflated Metallica went back to New York for its next concert on the 20th at J. Bee's Rock III. The band shared the bill with Anthrax, who let the Four Horsemen use their backline.

Previous page: Metallica backstage after their first concert in the Netherlands at the Aardschok festival in Isselhal (Zwolle), 11 February 1984.

SEVEN DATES OF HELL
3 February–29 August 1984

The Seven Dates of Hell tour began at the Volkhaus in Zürich, Switzerland. Unsurprisingly, things got out of hand, as a member of staff recalls. 'Metallica went fuckin' *nuts* on the first night. What had happened was, there were some fans outside, and one of Metallica had broken a window to get to the fans and say hello. By this time the promoters had decided that they were gonna kill them for damaging the venue, so we brought them into our dressing room. [...] They just sat there like little rabbits caught in the headlights.' After this dramatic start, the tour moved to Milan, then Nuremberg, Paris and the Netherlands, wrapping up at the Poperinge festival in Belgium, where Venom had a few end-of-tour pranks ready for Metallica before they went on stage. 'Some of the road crew had covered Lars's drum heads in talcum powder. And we were throwing fruit at them, it was just high jinks.'

At the end of the tour, the two bands went their separate ways, and Metallica drove to Copenhagen to record "Ride the Lightning" at the Sweet Silence studios. The recording session was split into two due to studio availability, and the band was free for a few weeks. No rest for the wicked, though. Instead of taking some time out, the four Americans managed to book a few dates in England, and jetted off to give two concerts at the Marquee Club in London on 14 and 27 March. These were sellout shows, and the band was a hit. The future looked bright for Metallica in Europe.

Hit the Lights
The Four Horsemen
Phantom Lord
Creeping Death
Ride the Lightning
When Hell Freezes Over
(The Call Of Ktulu Demo Version)
Seek & Destroy
(Anesthesia) Pulling Teeth
Whiplash
Metal Militia

FROM THE HEAVY SOUND FESTIVAL...
Poperinge, Belgium · 10 June 1984

This unforgettable gig was one of the very first in Europe dedicated entirely to hard rock and metal music. The line-up at the Heavy Sound festival included big names like Motörhead, Mercyful Fate and Twisted Sister alongside supporting acts H-Bomb, Lita Ford, Faithful Breath and Barón Rojo. Lars, Kirk and James have fond memories of this concert with its famous strong Belgian beer and the 'funny smell of cigarettes'. Beyond the myths, this was an important gig, because the Belgian crowd got to see a furious Metallica unleashing their wrath on stage. The bootleg recordings made at the time give some insight into just how fast the band played "Hit the Lights"! On that day, Cliff was on top of his game, and the band had no problem playing alongside heavyweights Motörhead and Twisted Sister.

Kirk and James, two thrash legends.

Hit the Lights
The Four Horsemen
Phantom Lord
No Remorse
Ride the Lightning
Seek and Destroy
(Anesthesia) Pulling Teeth
Whiplash

... TO THE BREAKING SOUND FESTIVAL
Le Bourget, France · 29 August 1984

Many French metalheads consider this festival to be a founding moment, and for good reason. The bill included an incredible number of bands that were already ultra-famous at the time: Ozzy Osbourne, Gary Moore, Mötley Crüe, Metallica, Accept (on the Wednesday) and Dio, Mercyful Fate and Uli Roth (on the Thursday), with a special guest, the legendary Blue Öyster Cult! At the time, metal was becoming hugely popular in France and fans swarmed through the gates. There were no toilets or showers and nowhere to camp. It took hours to get a beer and the organizing team was completely overwhelmed. To top it off, Accept and Mercyful Fate, as well as some others, cancelled their appearance. Beer cans were thrown on stage by disappointed fans, but the Four Horsemen showed up on time, ready to play. Despite the sound quality that some French fans described as 'disgusting', James pulled through, violently headbanging throughout his performance. This first metal festival also gave fans an opportunity to get closer to the group during autograph-signing sessions and as they mixed with the crowd. The band were a roaring success!

'The studio is just a labour. Getting on stage is the reward,' says Cliff Burton, here on stage at the Breaking Sound Festival in Le Bourget in August 1984.

BANGING THE HEAD THAT DOESN'T BANG: THE MARATHON TOUR
16 November–20 December 1984

This endless tour began on 16 November 1984 in Rouen, France, and took the band (supported by Tank) to many European countries – Belgium, France, Italy, Switzerland, Germany, the Netherlands, Denmark (Lars's home country), Sweden, Finland, finishing in London, England. From 1983 the band got its act together, and James got even more confident and reckless on stage. Though he started out rather shy, he had now mastered the shout/sung vocal style so typical of metal bands at the time. Between tracks, his taunts were now more convincing than ever, he was the boss. That confident attitude fitted perfectly with the spirit of "Ride the Lightning", an extremely tense record with a snare drum sound that snaps like a bullet. When James, Cliff and Kirk launched into perfectly coordinated headbanging, the audience followed their lead; a symbiosis was created between the musicians and their fans.

RIDE THE LIGHTNING TOUR: RETURN TO THE HOMELAND
10 January–31 December 1985

After a break for Christmas in San Francisco and LA, Metallica kicked off the first leg of its US tour with WASP and Armored Saint, starting in New York then heading north, then west (Hartford, Philadelphia, Baltimore, Montreal, Ottawa, Buffalo, Toronto, New York, Columbus, Cincinnati, Indianapolis, Detroit, Madison, Minneapolis, Cleveland, Milwaukee and Green Bay). Their journey took them through the Deep South to Texas, where countless eager fans were waiting. The aim of the tour was to share tracks from the latest album with as many people as possible. John Bush, the singer of Armored Saint, remembers: 'We toured with Metallica on the RTL tour, when we had "March of the Saint" out. It was a really new, fresh, incredible time for that kind of music.'

Brian TATLER

'It just seemed so, well, not just complex, but they were such long songs, with loads of tight bits and little details that they must have spent ages on. I was impressed with the musicianship, but the songwriting just seemed like a bit of a wall flying at me at 100 miles per hour!'

Fight Fire With Fire
Ride the Lightning
Phantom Lord
The Four Horsemen
(Anesthesia) Pulling Teeth
For Whom The Bell Tolls
No Remorse
Fade to Black
Seek & Destroy
Whiplash
Creeping Death
Guitar Solo
Am I Evil? (Diamond Head Cover)
Motorbreath

The pace was hectic and the concerts bigger than ever (Metallica was now headlining), so the band decided to take a break from May to July 1985. But as usual, the four musicians played the long game and were soon hard at work on their next project: a third album. Entitled *Master of Puppets*, it went on to be the ultimate thrash record; an unrivalled monument to the genre, adored by millions of fans around the world. The record finally allowed Metallica to fulfil the dream they had had since the very beginning: to be the kings of metal.

PEAK THRASH

This new chapter in the lives of the Four Horsemen was one of the most important in their incredible story. The band made a record that redefined metal and opened the doors to huge venues where they played to sellout audiences all over the world. It was also a sad time for the musicians, who had to deal with the tragic death of Cliff Burton, a catastrophic event whose effects are palpable in their next record, ...*And Justice for All*: a cold and almost surgical album that echoed the young mens' grief.

At this pivotal moment when the vibrancy of their huge and elaborate concerts contrasted with the sadness coating their personal lives, the Metallica boys became men and established thrash as the most popular metal style for years to come. Jason Newsted brought a breath of fresh air to the band and its performances, as well as his unique personality. But Metallica faced adversity again when James had an accident and was forced to give up the guitar and miss some of their cult concerts, like Donington Park on 22 August 1987.

DAMAGE INC. TOUR

Master of Puppets came out on 21 February 1986, and it was a huge challenge as well as an immense opportunity for Metallica. In addition to the album's promotional tour, the band was chosen to open the American shows given by Ozzy Osbourne, the famous Black Sabbath vocalist, who was at the height of his fame. Metallica had a double marathon to run in the spring of 1986.

ON TOUR WITH KING OZZY
27 March–3 August 1986

It was no coincidence that the band found themselves on tour with one of the greatest heavy metal stars of all time, Ozzy Osbourne! They had gone to the next level in terms of their stage performances, as Jeff Dunn from Venom recalls, after a memorable Metallica show on 14 September 1986 at the Loreley MetalFest in the FRG (Federal Republic of Germany): 'The first time I knew Metallica were gonna be huge was at the Loreley Festival. We were headlining and they were just beneath us. I remember being backstage and hearing them playing "Seek & Destroy" and the

whole audience singing it. Then James shouting, "What the fuck was that!" And then the whole place going mad. James had that rapport with the audience, they were his that night. It was that point I can honestly say that Metallica were starting to overtake us, that was the European gig where they definitely made their mark.'

Opposite: On 14 June 1986, Metallica open for Ozzy Osbourne at Long Beach Arena (California)
Above: The Four Horsemen and Ozzy Osbourne (centre) backstage during the Damage Inc. Tour

THE FOUR-STRING VIRTUOSO

Clifford Lee Burton was born in upmarket Castro Valley, California, on 10 February 1962. He had two older siblings, Scott and Connie. He was an active and lively child, playing baseball, fishing and hunting in the holidays. He also loved making music with his friends. In 1978, a teenage Cliff started bass lessons. He was quickly scouted by local bands and his musicianship and (already) endearing personality made him a popular player. Naturally calm, Cliff was surprisingly enthusiastic when it came to his interests, and utterly determined to achieve the goals he set for himself. When he started taking lessons, he made such incredible progress that before long he was a better player than his teacher!

He was fascinated by classical composers such as Bach and Beethoven, but mainly drawn to heavy metal and punk. That combination of interests perfectly characterized Cliff's playing style: he fused the raw wildness of modern music with the virtuoso melodies of those classical composers. A perfect example is the long bass solo in "(Anesthesia) Pulling Teeth", which lifted his bass from a support act for thrash guitar to the star attraction. There is no doubt in anyone's mind that he transformed the Metallica sound. And his relaxed personality helped to keep the other members of the band on an even keel. Cliff was a natural artist.

He was also an excellent songwriter, very determined, and respected by those around him for his talent and commitment. For many early fans, his time with Metallica was a "golden age". Many see the bassist as the vital element that had been missing from the line-up.

AT PROVIDENCE CIVIC CENTER: CONFIRMATION

Providence, Rhode Island · 23 April 1986

This huge tour allowed the band to veer away from pure thrash and cast its net to a much wider audience, though its steamroller set list was designed to get the heavy metal crowd on board right from the start. Unsurprisingly, the hammering hit "Battery" opened the show with a triumphant, powerful and ultra-melodic kick-off. With the first epic notes of the intro done, the thrash cavalcade sprang into action and the fans were putty in their hands.

Next up – and in the same pulsating vein – was the second track from their record. The audience was hysterical when James leant over his microphone, hair in his eyes, and screamed the title of the song. He launched into "Master of Puppets" with its now-legendary opening riff: relentless cut-throat thrash, the band's hallmark. The chemistry was perfect between Kirk and the frontman, and the two guitars alternated the epic opening bars with devilish precision, supported by thrusts from Lars as he fiercely bashed the life out of his cymbals. Cliff joined the headbanging frenzy, flying the flag of House Metallica in his iron fist. The mixture of typical metal savagery (headbanging, howling, boisterousness) and the band's unmatched precision was astounding. That evening, the crowd was with Metallica all the way, screaming and yelling themselves hoarse. At the core of this fiendishly effective set were the band's hits, selected to drive the audience wild.

That same chemistry persisted throughout the tour and the band was given a warm and enthusiastic welcome by a crowd who had come primarily to see Ozzy Osbourne.

In almost two months, they performed 35 concerts on this marathon tour. The list of states is long: Kansas, Oklahoma, Missouri, Michigan, Illinois, Wisconsin, Indiana, Ohio, Pennsylvania, New York, Maryland, New Jersey, Rhode Island, Connecticut, Massachusetts, North Carolina, Tennessee, Louisiana, Texas, New Mexico, Colorado, Utah and Arizona. But even that enormous undertaking couldn't satisfy the band. They were hungry for more, and performed this same series of shows throughout the summer, before taking a detour to Europe to play for their adoring fans who just hadn't been able to get enough since "Ride the Lightning".

Battery
Master Of Puppets
Welcome Home (Sanitarium)
For Whom The Bell Tolls
Ride The Lightning
Creeping Death
Am I Evil?
Damage, Inc.

Serious
staging

Metallica took things to the next level on this tour. Until now, they had been focusing on energy, shouting at the crowd and getting close to their fans. Their concerts now took place in huge stadiums or halls and the band needed a different approach. This tour had a full-on set design with real staging and impressive scenery, it was a spectacle for the audience. To promote *Master of Puppets* and remedy the fact that the band now performed in large venues where they simply couldn't get close to their fans, the stage was set up using visual elements from the album cover and divided into two parts. There was a raised area at back of the stage for Lars and his drum kit so that the audience could see him play, even from right at the back. The second area – where the other three players would perform – spanned the entire width of the stage, and extended to the area where Lars played. Cliff and his bass were on the right, while Kirk stood on the left. Frontman James obviously took centre stage.

The set design was inspired by the *Master of Puppets* album cover, starting with the white crosses that flanked Lars and his drum kit. They were identical to those on the record, and made it seem like the band was moving through a cemetery. The show was lit using the same shades as those on the cover: red, orange and ochre, bathing the stage in a dusky glow. For the first time ever, Metallica treated its fans to a full-on spectacle, and kept the showmanship high, right through to the end. When the first notes of the famous riff from "Master of Puppets" rang out, the three perfectly aligned musicians launched into coordinated headbanging, adding the power of movement to the violence of sound.

NASHVILLE MUNICIPAL AUDITORIUM: JAMES (ALMOST) OUT OF THE PICTURE
Nashville, Tennessee · 27 July 1986

When the Metallica boys returned, they got straight back on the road for a new leg of gigs in the US. Just before one of those – in Evansville, Indiana – James Hetfield had a skateboarding accident and broke his wrist. That night's gig was cancelled and James wore a cast until September. Metallica didn't let that stop them. John Marshall, the guitarist in Metal Church, stepped up, skilfully replacing him on rhythm guitar. But there was no way that a newcomer was going to take the limelight! Strangely, Marshall played from behind the scenes during the first few concerts.

'The first six gigs I played in 86 were opening for Ozzy, and I stood off to the side of the stage where the audience couldn't see me. James would introduce me after about two songs or so. The rest of the gigs that year were in Europe and the UK. I was sort of off to the side where the audience could see me, but kind of in the background. After a few gigs Cliff would motion for me to stand more on stage, and eventually I was onstage every night.'

Even though he replaced James without a hitch, John remembers just how nervous he was about taking on the huge challenge: 'The hard part was trying to match the vibe and intensity of his guitar playing. I knew how to play the riffs and song arrangements OK, but getting the feel right was difficult. It was also hard because the rest of the band follows his voice and guitar onstage. I wasn't used to that type of situation. I think I was more worried about what the rest of the band thought, than what the audience thought... The first time I played I literally had to learn the songs overnight, so I didn't have much time to think about it.'

Left: John Marshall replaces James Hetfield while he is recovering from his accident in July 1986.
Opposite: Cliff Burton during a concert at the UIC Pavilion in Chicago on 5 April 1986. The set design includes elements from the cover of Master of Puppets.

ON THE ROAD WITH ARMORED SAINT
23 May–7 June 1986

Alongside this long series of concerts with Ozzy, Metallica also began another tour supported by Armored Saint, a band that, although it does enjoy a speedy double-pedal cavalcade, plays a brand of metal that is clearly heavier than our favourite titans of thrash. The two bands began their epic journey on 23 May 1986 in Tulsa, Oklahoma before continuing to Missouri, Illinois, Iowa, Minnesota, Wisconsin, Nebraska and Texas, playing a total of 11 shows in just two weeks.

BLASTING INTO EUROPE WITH ANTHRAX
10–26 September 1986

Metallica (with John Marshall) completed its monster US tour alongside Ozzy Osbourne in the autumn of 1986. The band then flew to Europe, where they gave a monumental show at London's Hammersmith Odeon with Anthrax, another thrash icon from the USA.

John
MARSHALL

'I remember the crowd reaction usually being positive. After all, it was still Metallica, just with one more guy onstage!'

HAMMERSMITH ODEON: BACK TO EUROPE IN STYLE
London, England · 21 September 1986

The Anthrax guitarist Ian Scott remembers that special night: 'We really felt that we were part of something; the crowds were crazy and we really felt as if there was something happening. The energy was palpable.'

This first leg in the United Kingdom gave Metallica a chance to cover lots of cities: Cardiff, Bradford, Edinburgh, Dublin, Belfast, Manchester, Sheffield, Newcastle, Birmingham and of course, London. Again, the band was hugely successful, reaping the benefits of previous tours from fans who could still remember their concerts. Many of them cite this series of shows as launching the thrash metal wave in the UK.

SOLNAHALLEN: JAMES IS BACK!
Stockholm, Sweden · 26 September 1986

Faithful to its motto: 'play everywhere as much as possible', Metallica then headed to Northern Europe, starting in Sweden this time, with their fellow Americans, Anthrax. Even though John performed brilliantly at every gig, James was getting impatient, and felt that his wrist was almost healed. The concert at the Solnahallen in Stockholm was a great opportunity to find out. James was pumped and raced to attack the stage with his trusty white Explorer guitar. The band kept John Marshall on as a roadie just in case James had not completely recovered. Luckily, the newly reformed band gave an impeccable show, led by James who was on top form! For many Cliff Burton admirers, this gig was one of the bravest for the bassist, who admirably interpreted the American national anthem, "The Star-Spangled Banner", with virtuoso tapping sequences and supercharged bends.

Metallica gave a flawless performance and the tight-knit group left the Swedish capital late at night to travel to Lars's homeland, Denmark, where the next concert was to take place.

killed in crash

LJUNGBY, Sweden (AP) — A member of the American rock group Metallica was killed and the eight other band members were injured Saturday when their van crashed on an icy road, police reported.

They said Clifford Lee Burton, the 24-year-old bassist for the heavy-metal group, was killed, but they did not have any further information about him.

The group was travelling in a British-registered van from a concert in Stockholm to Copenhagen, Denmark, when the accident occurred in southern Sweden.

The British driver and eight surviving band members — six Americans — work on a new...
...worked on ne...
...away and reha...
...vels, and with...
...ight was to s...
...d with new...
...auditions Gig...
...set of Europ...
...be ground-br...
...marketing pie...
...the biggest...
...ycler newsp...
...ca after a s...
...try. After...
...went cra...
...rauma an...
...ing to New...
...e boys i...
...es of The Four Hors...
...their second album Ride The...
...stry maturing at an alarming rate of knots, clas...
...Fire and Creeping Death O Prime Management an...
...the bands stature rapidly grew. In late 198...

A NIGHTMARE COMES TRUE CLIFF BURTON...

It is nearly dawn on September the 27th. Two... buses drive along a remote stretch of the E4 be... the Swedish towns of Vämama and Ljungby. It is... The sun is trying to peek over the densely pa... forests. Suddenly, one of the drivers turns his ste... column sharply to the right, crossing the central re... vation. The bus ends its journey eighteen metres on... the opposite lane. The bus is on its side. People a... screaming. This is Metallica's tour bus. Cliff Burton... Clifford Lee Burton, 24 years old and an America... citizen, is dead.

The Metallica fans around the world... weren't the only ones puzzled about... that happened. The Swedish Police,... o, had little idea what went on. One... rsion of the events is the driver's. He... ntains that he saw ice on the road... d swerved to avoid it. When quest... ed by the Police, he said that there... no chance of him being tired. But... ots were cast on his story when the... ish Police checked the road... diately after the accident and... no sign of ice. The 48-year-old... was arrested and charged with... nt driving, leading to the death... ssenger.
k of ice isn't the only flaw in the... s reconstruction of the acci... cording to the second driver,... no way that the accused had... had enough sleep. Yet the driver of the... Metallica bus still maintains that... here saw the driver stopped for a break, I think...

Police find any mechanical fault on... bus. The bus was only three years... and even the accused said that the... had never been any problems with... Whether the bus driver is to blame o... whether there was a mechanical fault... doesn't change what happened - Cliff... Burton will never stand on stage again... All that remains for the survivors is... shock. The rest of the band were lucky... No serious injuries just cuts, bruises... and deep shock. Drummer Lars Ulrich... broke a toe and Tour Manager Bobby... Schneider dislocated his shoulder that... had to be treated in hospital.
In a telephone interview shortly after... the accident, Lars Ulrich gave this... account of what happened.
"We left Stockholm round about mid... night. We were all kinda tired and fell... asleep within minutes. At some point,... the bus stopped for a break, I think... must have been...

48 year old busdriver... taken into...

Sista intervjun med CLIFF BURTON i METALLICA
—Jag hoppas få råd med ett eget hem och en dag även spela lugnare musik...

OKEJs Ulf Magnusson tog sista bilden på Cliff Burton.

Sista bilden på Metallica med Cliff Burton.

—JAG VISSTE INTE ATT CLIFF VAR DÖD

Cliff Burton wurde durch die Windschutzscheibe geschleudert und überrollt. Er war auf der Stelle tot.

Vom Verlust des Freundes gezeichnet: Metallica und Tourmanager Bobby Schneider (rechts), der sich bei dem Unfall eine Schulter ausgerenkt hat. Links Lars Ulrich, für den der Unfall mit einem gebrochenen Zeh und einem Schock endete.

To the Hammer of Metal!
NOW CLIFF IS PLAYING THE WILDEST BASS IN HEAVEN!

Cliff Burton ist tot! Das ganze zwei Tage vor dem Tour-Beginn in Deutschland. Alle Headbanger in Deutschland, auch in der ganzen Welt, sind erschüttert. Der wohl wildeste Bassist, der Hallen und Arenen erzittern ließ, ist nicht mehr am Leben!
Den Bangern hier im Kreis Osnabrück, und den Bangern in der ganzen Welt wohl auch, geht es saumäs. Heute ist Donnerstag! Es ist 21.30 Uhr. Wo ich mich jetzt hineinsuche, kann sich jeder vorstellen? Ich habe vorhin, um 20.00 Uhr, fast Tränen in die Augen bekommen. Jetzt sollte das Spektakel hier losgehen.
Aber irgend etwas war dagegen.
Cliff lebt nicht mehr und alle Banger trauern um "Metallica".
Ich glaube, im Namen aller Headbanger zu sprechen, wenn ich sage: "Metallica muß weiterleben, auch wenn es nie mehr so werden wird, wie es einmal war!!"
A sad hello to "Metallica" and all the Heavy Metal which is in this fucking world!

Markus Weckermann
Graf-Stauffenberg-Str. 47
Osnabrück

OBITUARY   ROLLING STONE

has made it, over the course of three albums, the biggest-selling group of its ilk. The band had just kicked off a continental tour with a concert in Stockholm and were en route to a date in Copenhagen when, at about 6:15 a.m., the tour bus apparently went into a skid, and Burton — who, like the other three band members, was asleep — was thrown out of a window. The bus then tipped over on its side, crushing the bassist to death. Lars Ulrich, the drummer for the San Francisco Bay Area band, sustained a minor injury, and the group's road manager suffered a dislocated shoulder. Metallica's European tour was immediately canceled.

Metallica was at a high point in its career: its second album, *Ride the Lightning*, sold more than 500,000 copies in the U.S., and its third and latest LP, *Master of Puppets*, has sold 750,000 copies worldwide and is still going strong. Metallica was scheduled to begin a series of U.S. concerts at the end of October. The status of those dates was unknown at press time, but according to comanager Cliff Burnstein, "They're going to want to work. I don't think this band's going to fall apart."

— *Kurt Loder*

CLIFF BURTON: 1962-1986

CLIFF BURTON, BASSIST WITH THE PREmier new-metal band Metallica, was killed in a tour-bus crash in Ljungby, Sweden, on September 27th. He was twenty-four.
Metallica's combination of heavy-metal guitar power and punk-rock velocity — a fusion known as "thrash" —

CLIFF BURTON

The road to death:
The Burton tragedy

The crew travelled on two buses. The first carried stage equipment (instruments, amps and the set). The second was for the musicians, technicians and roadies. That night, the second bus led the way towards Denmark. Everyone on board was in their bunks, making the most of a few hours' rest while the bus motored along the E4 between the Swedish towns of Ljungby and Värnamo. A little before 7 a.m., most of the passengers were fast asleep when a terrible accident occurred. John Marshall, now a roadie, remembers: 'Apparently the bus drifted off to the right side of the road, and the driver steered left to correct. As he did this, the back end of the bus spun out to the right. While this was happening, I remember waking up, being bounced out of the bunk because the tyres were "chattering" as the bus skidded. [...] By the time it stopped, the bus was on the right side of the road, facing the other direction. As it slid into the right shoulder of the road, it caught the gravel and tipped onto its right side. When the bus tipped, the two rows of bunks collapsed together, trapping guys underneath. [...] I remember sitting out on the ground, waiting for help, just stunned at being awakened this way, and trying to take it all in. Bobby Schneider, the tour manager, was still inside the bus, helping to get the guys out.'

A few moments later, all the occupants had managed to untangle themselves from the wreckage, and Kirk and James, who were stunned but escaped with only minor injuries, came to their senses. As he moved away from the scene of the accident, James heard screams coming from the back of the bus. Stepping closer, he saw two legs under a blanket, sticking out from under the wreckage. It was Cliff Burton, who had died at the scene.

In shock, James immediately tried to find out what had happened: 'I saw the bus lying right on him. I saw his legs sticking out. I freaked. The bus driver, I recall, was trying to yank the blanket out from under him to use for other people. I just went, "Don't you fucking dare do that!" I already wanted to kill the guy. I don't know if he was drunk or if he hit some ice. All I knew was, he was driving and Cliff wasn't alive any more.'

When the ambulance arrived, everyone on the bus was taken to hospital and a crane was used to lift the wreckage and free Cliff's body. According to initial reports, Cliff was thrown from his bunk during the accident, flew through the window and was killed when the bus landed on its side.

The band was devastated. They decided to spend the night at a hotel in Ljungby, where James drowned his sorrows in booze, and in a fit of rage broke two of the windows in his room. Kirk and Lars were deep in shock; they slept with the light on all night.

TOUGH JOURNEY HOME
October–November 1986

This tragedy at the height of their fame left the band in a dazed limbo. One of its pillars was suddenly missing, they had all lost a friend. The band found themselves with a difficult choice to make: should they quit making music as Metallica out of respect for Cliff or continue what he built in his memory? Brian Slagel remembers: 'What happened was, about three or four weeks after the accident I got a call from Lars, who said, "Well, we need a new bass player." So I said, "I think I got the guy for you..."'

Kirk explains their eagerness to replace Cliff: 'Right after the accident happened, we were very traumatized, and felt a lot of emotional distress over the situation. The worst thing we could do is just sit in our room and sulk over the matter and wallow in our pity. [...] We each thought individually, we have to keep on going, we have to work because it wouldn't be fair to Cliff to just stop. [...] He would've wanted us to go on.'

METALLICA RETURNS TO THE RESEDA COUNTRY CLUB
Reseda, California · 8 November 1986

Barely a week after officially joining Metallica, Jason Newsted got ready to take his first steps on stage with his new band at the Country Club in Reseda, California, on 8 November 1986. The band didn't want to attract a big crowd for its first show after the tragedy, so kept a low profile and limited publicity. That evening, they played a set of 13 tracks from three of their albums and Jason was on fire. He channelled his fierce energy into effortlessly controlling riffs and thrash combinations. He was effective and discreet, striking the perfect tone. Cliff was still at the forefront of everyone's minds, and it would have been wrong to seek to replace him with an exuberant performer.

Kirk HAMMETT

'*Right after the accident happened, we individually decided that the best way to get rid of all our frustrations would be to hit the road and get all the anxiety and frustrations out on stage, where they should go. They should go towards a positive thing like that.*'

MORE THAN A REPLACEMENT

JASON NEWSTED

Jason Curtis Newsted was born on 4 March 1963 in Battle Creek, Michigan, but spent most of his childhood in Niles.

In 1977, the Newstad family moved to a farm in Kalamazoo with their four children. Jason spent most of his time playing sports and taking care of his beloved horses. Even though music wasn't one of the family's main interests, Jason grew up to the sounds of the Jackson Five and the Newsted family favourite: the Osmonds. The famous Gibson guitar factory was close to the Newsted family home. Despite satisfactory grades, Jason left high school before getting his diploma and began learning an instrument. He set his sights on the bass, but didn't do very well. He then tried the piano but wasn't thrilled with that either. Being a keen admirer of Gene Simmons, the bassist from Kiss, he eventually went back to the bass.

His second attempt at picking up the instrument was more successful, and he earned a spot in his first band, alongside his bass teacher. Jason was a hard worker and proved to be a good and conscientious musician. He was a member of Flotsam and Jetsam when he was asked to audition for Metallica. In just a few days, he managed to master their entire repertoire and joined the band. Jason played bass for Metallica until 2001, when he threw in the towel, visibly exhausted by the band's countless unresolved problems after Cliff's death, from which he said he suffered all the time he was with the band. He went on to form Echobrain, joined the sci-fi thrash outfit Voivod and finally created Newsted, his own band, in which he still plays.

INTEGRATION TOURS

Jason quickly took his first steps on stage as Metallica's keenly awaited bassist. Little did he know what the months spent on the road would be like alongside Lars, James and Kirk! Metallica was still on the rise and, backstage, the young musicians were revelling in the rock-star life and the overindulgence that goes with it. On the second leg of the Damage Inc. Tour, Jason found out what the members of Metallica were really like – schoolboy pranks that smacked of inner malaise, hazing of all varieties. The new bassist went through a baptism of fire. But he passed with flying colours, partly thanks to his impeccable, metronomic performance on stage that met the high expectations of Lars and James...

Jason NEWSTED

'It was a test all the time – wind-ups from everyone to see if I could cut it. Everybody would go down to the bar to have sushi and sake for days and charge it to my room. [...] This went on for a year. If I was going to buckle, they had to know. I took it and that was that.'

METALLICA IN JAPAN:
JASON JOINS THE RANKS
15–20 November 1986

A few days after the first performance with his new band, Jason prepared for an in-depth Metallica experience; a tour around Japan from 15 to 20 November. It was an opportunity for the musicians to get closer and create some memories with their new bassist. While their on-stage cohesion seemed perfect, with Jason performing as well during the shows in Tokyo and Nagoya as he did in San Francisco, behind the scenes the atmosphere was somewhat different…

James, Lars and Kirk decided to make the tour a sort of hazing process for the newcomer before he could be brought in permanently. Metallica's famous photographer Ross Halfin remembers how it went: 'We'd all pick on him. We'd all get a cab and make him get a cab on his own. We'd sign all the room bills to his room. This was before they had money… They used to really, really pick on him. It started off as a joke and then it got really beyond a joke. One of the first ones was that they'd all slept with me and that I was gay, and that he should too if he wanted to stay in the band. And he was actually worried about it for a while. I'm serious!'

Jason also remembers the transition after the Japan tour: 'One time, it's four in the morning, they're hammered and knocking on my hotel door when we were in New York. "Get up motherfucker! It's time to drink, pussy!" You know? "You're in Metallica now! You better open that fucking door!" They kept pounding. Kaboom! The door frame shreds, and the door comes flying in. And they go, "You should have answered the door, bitch!" They grab the mattress and flip it over with me on it. They put the chairs, the desk, the TV stand – everything in the room – on top of the mattress. They threw my clothes, my cassette tapes, my shoes out the window. Shaving cream all over the mirrors, toothpaste everywhere. Just devastation. They go running out the door, "Welcome to the band, dude!"'

It was mostly good-natured, but Jason was quick to catch on that the constant bullying was in fact a symptom of the sadness the band had felt since Cliff died. Getting back on the road so quickly with a new member probably didn't give Lars and James (in particular) time to process what had happened and come to terms with the death of their beloved bassist. They would have to wait a little longer for that much-needed respite, because having just touched down from Japan, Metallica was getting ready for a new set of dates in the United States.

Opposite: James, Jason, Lars and Kirk during a photo shoot at a hotel in Tokyo, November 1986.
Above: At Shibuya Public Hall in Tokyo, on 15 November 1986.

BACK TO NORTH AMERICA: THE METALLICA EXPRESS!
3–19 December 1986

Barely having time to turn around after their Japanese ex-travaganza, Metallica hit the road again on 28 November for a gig in Poughkeepsie, New York, before touring the East Coast and Canada. They were welcomed with open arms during sellout shows in New Jersey, Quebec, Ontario, Vancouver and Oregon. Neither was there an empty seat in the house on 2 January when they came home to San Francisco and wrapped up the tour.

A TRIUMPH IN EUROPE: COMING FULL CIRCLE
8 January–30 August 1987

They then set their sights back on Europe, having fled the continent just a few months before. This time, the band was determined to go east and conquer some new territory! A new tour was planned, starting off with a show in Copenhagen, which had been cancelled in September 1986 after Cliff passed away. This time, Metallica was supported by another iconic thrash band: Metal Church. The two bands toured the Old Continent throughout the winter of 1987, giving six concerts in France (Nice, Clermont-Ferrand, Strasbourg, Lyon, Bordeaux and Paris). The most legendary performance happened at the Zénith, in the French capital.

PARIS ZENITH: THE INDUCTION OF JASON NEWSTED
Paris, France · 5 February 1987

Metallica flooded the venue with guitar feedback at the start of the gig, banging out "Battery", then "Master of Puppets" with James shrieking at the crowd: 'All right Paris! Deal with the "Master of Puppets"!' The highlight of this gig was the long bass solo by Jason Newsted. Jason delivered a spine-tingling performance worthy of the greatest heavy metal guitar solos. Pick in hand and foot to the floor on his distortion and flanger pedals, Jason showed the French crowd that he was as talented a musician as his predecessor. The audience loved him, and the specialist press were in ecstasy. As a sign that Jason's hazing period was over, at the end of "Master of Puppets", James introduced him to the audience – who gave him a standing ovation – before roaring into "For Whom the Bell Tolls". For many of the fans, the intense night would go down in history, and several bootleg recordings soon passed from hand to hand. The tour wrapped on 13 February 1987 with a concert in Sweden, and the band headed back to the States. They returned to Europe in August 1987 for four concerts, including three as part of the gigantic Monsters of Rock festival in Germany and England.

In early 1987, the band heads east on its conquest of Europe.

MONSTERS OF ROCK, DONINGTON PARK
Castle Donington, England
22 August 1987

The huge festival took place over three dates during the summer of 1987 and each time – once in the UK and two in the FRG – Metallica performed in front of more than 200,000 people! In England, the site chosen by festival promoter Paul Loadsby was the Donington Park motor-racing track in Leicestershire. For this ode to metal, Metallica shared the bill with Cinderella, W.A.S.P., Anthrax, Dio and the stars of Bon Jovi. It was an enormous park, and the stage was a gigantic scaffolding structure covered with backdrops in the colours of the bands that were set to perform.

Metallica were not the headliners (they appeared third on the bill), and they gave their performance in broad daylight. There was a striking contrast between their well-established indoor staging and the very raw feel of their outdoor performance. The lighting was limited, a large pit full of photographers separated the band from the audience, and the fans were crammed behind a long row of crash barriers... Despite everything, from the first notes of the instrumental intro, a forest of arms sprouted from the pit, welcoming the band as they entered the stage. The show kicked off with "Creeping Death", "For Whom the Bell Tolls" and "Fade to Black" (three top tracks from *Ride the Lightning*), the hit "Master of Puppets" was eighth on the set list. As for "Battery", which had often served as an effective opener, the band kept it back until the very end of the concert, as a third encore!

Just like in Paris a few months earlier, the fans at the festival that day felt that they had seen something very special. And as in Paris, many bootleg recordings were exchanged in secret long after everyone had gone home. After the two Monsters of Rock dates in Germany, the band flew back to the United States and didn't get back on stage again until 1988.

Castle Donington: the band performs on a bare stage in broad daylight. A chance to remember the Metallica of the early days!

DAMAGED JUSTICE TOUR: THE EPITOME OF THRASH

Metallica took a break in 1987 to focus on writing its new album, *...And Justice for All*. With its complex structures and surgical mixing, this record stands out for the almost complete absence of Jason's bass. It was the fourth album, and the guitars were at their peak. The mixes were overdone and the fans noticed the difficulties involved in transitioning from Cliff to Jason. Whatever! The band was still as hungry as ever and preparing to embark on a monumental new tour...

Blackened
For Whom the Bell Tolls
Welcome Home (Sanitarium)
The Four Horsemen
Harvester of Sorrow
Eye of the Beholder
Bass solo
Master of Puppets
Whiplash
One
Seek and Destroy
...And Justice for All

Creeping Death
Fade to Black
Guitar solo
Battery

Last Caress
Am I Evil?
Damage, Inc.

A MARATHON IN EUROPE
11 September–5 November 1988

Unsurprisingly, this epic journey was a triumph from the start. The band took in Hungary, Italy, Switzerland, Spain, France, the United Kingdom and Ireland. Danzig opened for Metallica on the first 14 dates, and James even sang backup on three tracks! On the second part of the tour, Danzig was replaced by Queensrÿche, the fathers of progressive metal, and the two bands travelled through Denmark, Finland, Sweden, Norway, the FRG, Belgium, taking another detour via France and the FRG again, before heading to the Netherlands where they took a break after the final show on 5 November.

Now international stars, the members of Metallica took more care with their stage outfits on this tour and decided to sport an understated look, avoiding the wardrobe mishaps of their early days. Gone were the bandoliers and mismatched outfits: Damaged Justice saw the band play head to toe in black, a perfect contrast with the immaculate whiteness of the statue that overlooked them. With the pressure off, Jason was more demonstrative and launched into the same furious headbanging as his band-

mates during the wildest riffs. And at the famous bridge in the middle of the flagship track "Blackened", the audience went into a trance, moving to the rhythm of the bass drum as Lars whipped up the crowd, marking the beat with his raised fist.

It was quite a different picture from the Metallica of old. Galvanized by the roars of the audience, the musicians roamed the stage like wild cats, occupying every square foot. They glared at the crowd, chins high, caged beasts ready to pounce. At some gigs, the band prowled onto the forestages that jutted out towards the audience. Lit by a single followspot, Kirk Hammett made good use of these while playing his solos, to get closer to the crowd. During "For Whom the Bell Tolls", James created an incredible connection with the crowd. While heavy chords resonated and Lars beat the pulse, he shouted at the spectators, commanding them to chant, 'Hey! Hey! Hey! Hey!' before resuming his legendary position, arched forward, one foot back, ready to attack!

Above: James Hetfield and Kirk Hammett, playing his black Custom Les Paul.

Staging

On 11 September 1988, Metallica set off on a yearlong world tour. This one was different from the others. For Damaged Justice, Metallica was clearly top of the bill. There was no way they were sharing the limelight and the other bands were clearly there to support them.

The tour took Metallica to new heights, and the spectacle kept on getting bigger. As with the previous tour, the main elements from the album cover were reproduced on stage. For Damaged Justice, there was an immense 20-foot reproduction of the allegory of justice from the artwork of ...And Justice for All. Standing majestic, high above the stage and the musicians, the decor certainly contributed to the show's visual appeal! The highlight of the performance was that the reproduction broke up gradually into smaller pieces. Metallica had the resources to do whatever they liked. They could now compete with big international names such as Motörhead, who brought a colossal bomber onto the stage, or Iron Maiden, who played every evening alongside a giant reproduction of their mascot, Eddie.

MONSTERS OF ROCK, *BIS REPETITA*
27 May–30 July 1988

Symbolizing the excesses of the music industry during the 80s, this legendary festival brought together five bands, the cream of the hard rock and metal crop: Metallica, Dokken, Kingdom Come, Scorpions and Van Halen. This immense and logistically complex machine attracted more than 50,000 people, who packed out the stadiums every evening. Because of the distances between dates and the time-consuming set-up and get-out processes, staging was limited to nothing more than a huge scaffold structure covered in black fabric. Only when darkness set did the typically 80s lighting effects bring some life to the stage. This truly was an epic show with more than nine hours of music on each date! Enthralled by this riot of content and the opportunity to see five metal bands in the same evening, the fans were beside themselves. Meanwhile the band members were in another world, whipped up by the cheering crowds, the follies of life on the road and incessant partying. Monsters of Rock incarnates a sort of apogee of American hard rock decadence during those years.

The immense metal promotion machine was set in motion on 27 May 1988 in Wisconsin. Then came Florida,

Washington DC, Massachusetts, Michigan, Pennsylvania, New York, Ohio, Maine, New Jersey, Texas, Tennessee, Missouri, Minnesota and California. Despite the adrenaline triggered by performing to a crowd at fever pitch every evening, James struggled to enjoy it all, he seemed to want to take a step back from the glitz of rock-star life. Lars looks back with fondness. 'It was fucking great. It was 88, right before *...And Justice for All* came out. [...] Basically, at that time, we used to start drinking when we woke up. We'd get the gig over by three o'clock, and then we'd have eight or nine hours to drink. It was awesome. This was our first exposure to big crowds, like, 50,000 people every day. Well, we were just drunk basically all the time. Girls knew we were part of the tour and wanted to fuck us, but at the same time we could blend in with the crowd. [...] Let's have another rum and Coke and go back in the audience and see what's happening. There are pictures of us at the top of Tampa Stadium with our pants off, flashing everybody. It's four o'clock in the afternoon and we're already drunk off our asses. The not-giving-a-fuck meter was peaking.' Despite their antics, Metallica kept performance levels high and perfectly reproduced the cold and aggressive

James
HETFIELD

'That whole tour was a big fog for me. Those were my Jägermeister days. It was bad coming back to some of those towns later, because there were a lot of dads and moms and husbands and boyfriends looking for me. Not good. People were hating me, and I didn't know why. That's when I realized Jägermeister is not the great elixir of life I thought it was.'

complexity of the latest album. While the anger of the repetitive thrash was still there, the band seemed to apply itself to playing these new, more complex pieces. Jason, who was getting a feel for huge stages, appeared perfectly at ease. Talkative Lars got his kicks by giving interviews from behind round smoked glasses, and never tired of telling stories about his exhilarating life on tour. The band members had arrived in the big league and could afford to do whatever they wanted. Sporting a shaggy beard and an evil grin, James was the ultimate frontman, and on this tour his voice reached an energetic and melodic maturity which became an integral part of the magical Metallica equation.

Monsters of Rock ended on 30 July 1988 with a concert in Denver, Colorado at Mile High Stadium, bringing a marathon of 28 gigantic shows to an end. Metallica had played for almost 1.5 million fans in less than two months!

James, Lars and Kirk at Rice Stadium (Houston, Texas) during the Monsters of Rock festival, 2 July 1988.

Creeping Death
For Whom the Bell Tolls
Harvester of Sorrow
Whiplash
Fade to Black
Seek and Destroy
Master Of Puppets

Last Caress
Am I Evil?
Battery

JUSTICE IN THE UNITED STATES
15 November 1988–21 April 1989

With its European conquest complete, the band returned home and once again got out on the road, taking in Ohio, Illinois, Wisconsin, Indiana, Michigan, Missouri, Oklahoma, New Mexico, Arizona, California, Utah and Colorado. In December, the band had a break to shoot the video for "One", a single from ...*And Justice for All*.

After a disappointment at the Grammy Awards where they hoped to win an award for best heavy metal band (Jethro Tull won in 1989), Metallica was fresher than ever and ready to go back on tour. They visited North Carolina, Georgia, New Jersey, Pennsylvania, New York, Maryland, Virginia, Massachusetts, Connecticut, Rhode Island, Maine and finally Canada. It was 21 April 1989, and this second part of the gruelling Damaged Justice tour came to an end.

JAPAN, THE PACIFIC, AMERICA: METALLICA IS EVERYWHERE!
1 May–7 October 1989

After trailing across North America for more than four months, the band could be forgiven for taking a welcome break. But the huge appetite of the metal industry was insatiable, so another series of dates in New Zealand, Australia, Japan, Hawaii and Alaska was planned, with The Cult as their support act.

When they returned to Japan, Metallica realized that they had become insanely popular. A cohort of young Japanese girls followed them around constantly, screaming the musicians' names and begging them to accept gifts: kitten toothbrushes, Snoopy-emblazoned napkins and photos of the band members leaving the bar the evening before... 'One evening when we returned to the hotel,' James remembers, 'a swarm of young girls threw themselves at us from a bush where they had been hiding, shouting and screaming: "Rars! Rars! Rars!"'

This long journey through the Pacific was followed by the final leg of the gargantuan tour, which began in September 1988. The band returned to the United States to perform in North Dakota, Minnesota, Iowa, South Dakota, Nebraska and over 30 other states! In October 1989, Damaged Justice finally came to an end, after three shows in Brazil, at venues in Rio de Janeiro and São Paulo.

Kirk Lee Hammett was named one of the 20 best guitarists of all time by the prestigious *Rolling Stone* magazine, and it's no surprise. His story began in El Sobrante, California on 18 January 1962. His father was an Irish army officer and his mother a Filipina public servant.

Although Kirk developed a passion for rock music at a very young age, unlike his future thrasher bandmates, he didn't spend hours practising his craft. He only started making serious music at the age of 15. A fan of Jimi Hendrix, Kiss and Aerosmith, he set his sights on the six-string to unravel the mystery of rock and get closer to his idols. He was a conscientious and dedicated learner right from the start, qualities that he revealed as soon as he joined Metallica, and that made it easier for him to fit in with his bandmates.

His determination to become an accomplished musician was evident when he made his debut using an amplifier he cobbled together inside a shoebox. He spent hours working in a Burger King restaurant to save for his first real Marshall amp.

In 1981, he formed the thrash band Exodus and shortly after began touring in the same venues as Metallica in their early days. After two years the band began to stagnate, and Kirk replied to Metallica when they got in touch with him to find a replacement for Dave Mustaine. The rest is history. Kirk's humanity and songwriting skills were a real breath of fresh air for the band, and he took its creative potential to a new level.

Calm, thoughtful and enthusiastic, he is still one of the strongest pillars in the group, despite the tribulations the Four Horsemen have faced during their long career.

ENDGAME AT ARENA IBIRAPUERA
São Paulo, Brazil · 7 October 1989

On 7 October 1989, the stage was in darkness as the first notes of "Blackened" rang out to open the show. Tension was running high and the screams of the hysterical crowd in the packed Ibirapuera stadium almost drowned out the sound. James, perched on the steps of the stage where Lars had his drum kit, began the furious riff of this incredible track. He was bathed in a greenish light, which then switched to the drum kit, just as Lars began hammering his snare.

When the track got properly under way, the now sophisticated light show illuminated the back of the stage, revealing a gigantic Roman-style stone wall reminiscent of the artwork from the band's most recent album. Like a devilish wild animal unleashed behind his drums, Lars battered his drums like they were pieces of artillery rather than percussion instruments.

The closing gig on the Damaged Justice tour was a representation of the band's journey around the world. Metallica was now a full-fledged musical giant. At the end of 1989, it was the only thrash band on the planet to be harassed by hordes of groupies, the only one to play three times in the same country in less than a few months and to sell out every evening, the only one to rally both fans of popular music and pure metalheads, the first to be nominated for the Grammys, the list was endless.

Drawn faces and palpable tension:
the gruelling tour takes its toll.

At the end of this humongous undertaking, James, Lars, Kirk and Jason had nothing left to give. This time they decided to take three months of well-deserved rest, and didn't get back on stage until the spring of 1990. Metallica then played a few dates in Europe and two concerts in stadiums in Toronto and New York with Aerosmith during the month of June. Aside from these rare appearances, the band focused on getting its strength back and above all, preparing a successor to ...And Justice for All. They went into the studio on 6 October 1990 and spent no fewer than eight months grafting hard on a pivotal album that is revered by some and reviled by others. Its official title is just *Metallica*, but it is better known by its nickname, the *Black Album*. A new chapter had begun...

THE CONSECRATION OF
THE GODS

Though the band's first records saw it rise to fame as a thrash band, far ahead of Slayer and the others, the *Black Album* – released on 13 August 1991 – marked a clear shift in the band's focus. Gone were the full-throated thrash onslaughts of "Ride the Lightning" and the double-pedal kicks of "Master of Puppets".

With a solid gold production by Bob Rock, this record had none of its predecessor's synthetic coldness. It exuded the smooth elegance of a band that had arrived at the pinnacle of its career. Its string of global hits didn't just intend to establish Metallica as the greatest thrash band of all time (arguably, in 1991, they already were), but quite simply the greatest rock band of the late 20th century.

And being a global band meant doing *ad hoc* tours, beginning with the immense Wherever We May Roam Tour, the gigantic stadiums of Monsters of Rock '91, the very stormy Guns N'Roses/Metallica Stadium Tour of 1992 and the apotheosis of 1993: the Nowhere Else to Roam Tour.

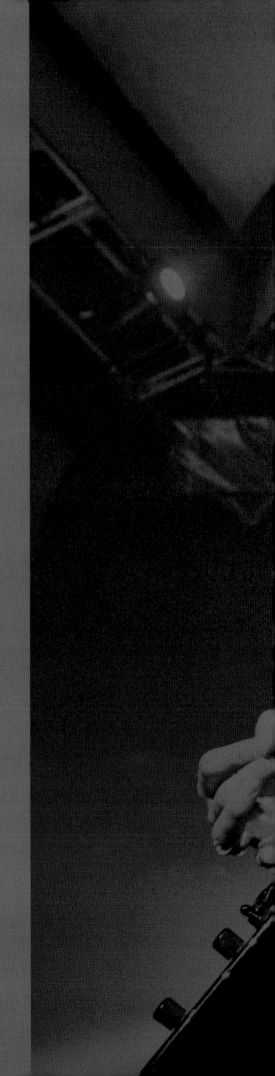

CONQUERING THE WORLD

Metallica began the Wherever We May Roam Tour on 1 August 1991, just two days after releasing the music video for "Enter Sandman", kicking off a journey that would span nearly a year and comprise 224 concerts. As the band does nothing by halves, Metallica also took part in a series of shows starting in August with the famous Monsters of Rock '91 alongside AC/DC, Mötley Crüe and Queensrÿche. Metallica wasn't just touring with one show, but now had to manage two simultaneous performances.

PHOENIX THEATER: A TASTER BEFORE THE BIG SHOW
Petaluma, California · 1 August 1991

Metallica got things going at the Phoenix Theater in Petaluma, California, with a set list that, curiously, included just two new tracks from its latest album: "Enter Sandman" and "Sad But True".

This time, the band preferred to draw from its older repertoire, putting together a live performance of 13 tracks still largely inspired by its 100 per cent thrash period. After the second show at the same place the next day, the band immediately took off for Europe to open the famous Monsters of Rock '91, the first date of which was in Copenhagen, in Lars Ulrich's native Denmark.

The *Black Album,* a determined shift

The famous *Black Album* is the quartet's first real controversial record. Instead of the pure thrash that fans expected to hear, it is full of midtempo hits, subtle arrangements, sometimes with strings and classical guitar. A million miles from thrash. Admittedly, it took eight months to produce and the perfectionist tendencies demonstrated by Lars (who sometimes spent several hours adjusting the tone of his snare drum before playing) hit new heights in the studio. Far from the wild spontaneity of *Ride the Lightning,* this album is the result of a long production process. For each track, James recorded three successive layers of rhythm guitar to accentuate the heavy aspect of the riffs! The highlight of the record – and a perfect example of the work accomplished on the album – is the ballad "Nothing Else Matters" with its string orchestration. For many early fans, this is the precise moment when the band began turning its back on its roots. For others, the extraordinary arrangement of this epic track is the highlight of the band's repertoire.

NO PLACE LIKE HOME: GENTOFTE STADION
Copenhagen, Denmark · 10 August 1991

Metallica played to a devoted crowd in a packed stadium, and James, hair blowing in the wind, announced "Sad But True" with an unsettling growl, playing the first thunderous chords of this downtempo hit with leaden riffs. As a tribute to the country where he was born, Lars had a Danish flag planted into his drum kit and was frenetic on his drums. The stage – immense, obviously – featured an immaculate white forestage, where Ulrich sat at his disproportionately wide white Tama drums. Dressed all in black (as had been the case since their last tour), the band delivered a flawless show with a sound quality that matched their most recent studio production: large, powerful and perfectly controlled. Metallica was back and seemed determined to conquer everything in its path.

BACK TO DONINGTON PARK
Castle Donington, England
17 August 1991

Still as part of the Monsters of Rock, the Four Horsemen came to England for one of the most legendary concerts on this tour.

That summer evening they were on top form, prowling around the stage with the help of a technological innovation that was making its debut: wireless amplification. Released from the constraints of the cables that connected their instruments to the amps, James, Jason and Kirk were clearly delighted to occupy the entire stage, and the fans lapped up their enjoyment.

Incessant headbanging, feet on the monitors or bass drum, aggressive grins and guitar necks raised to the sky: Metallica gave a memorable show that day, buoyed by James whose delightful energy even allowed him to take the liberty of interrupting "Harvester of Sorrow" with an impressive silence before picking up the assault-rifle pace.

In Copenhagen, Lars plants a Danish flag into his drum kit.

Magician, Bob Rock

Bob Rock was hugely important to Metallica's project. But, after countless setbacks while recording ...And Justice for All, the band hedged their bets, "booking" Flemming Rasmussen as well during the first month of work, in case things went wrong with Bob Rock. It was Flemming who saved the day during the mixing of the last record. Fortunately for everyone, Bob did what Bob does best, and everyone got along great. On the strength of his work with The Cult, Aerosmith and Mötley Crüe, Bob Rock was recognized as an effective producer who could give hard rock a powerful, precise character, with lots of bass. Metallica saw this mainstream touch as essential for their mix, to extend their audience beyond metal fans.

TUSHINO AIRFIELD:
TOTALLY OUTRAGEOUS

Moscow, Russia · 28 September 1991

After Hungary, the FRG, Switzerland, Belgium, the Netherlands, Austria, Italy, France and Spain, Monsters of Rock made a stop in Moscow for a concert on an unprecedented scale. The show took place at Tushino Airfield, a disused military air base. This was all happening two years after the fall of the Berlin Wall. The Soviet Union was collapsing, and Russians had only recently discovered Western rock culture. The promoters of Monsters of Rock had, of course, sniffed out the immense opportunity, welcoming close to a million fans to the site, who came to see the stars of Western hard rock and metal. The audience extended as far as the eye could see. The only landmarks for the musicians were the immense control tower that overlooked a sea of humanity, and the security helicopters that flew over the site regularly to keep an eye on things.

The Russian fans went berserk, reacting to each one of Hetfield's hecklings, under the sullen faces of the police and the sharp eye of the Russian army, who had come to keep order. Musically speaking, the concert was an enormous success, but there were countless injuries in the crowd due to poor management by the soldiers. This humongous concert marks the end of Monsters of Rock '91, which for many European fans remains the benchmark Metallica tour of the 90s.

The day after this memorable evening, the band took three weeks off before heading back on the road in the United States to continue the Wherever We May Roam Tour.

Metallica perform to 1.6 million fans in 1991. The immense crowd is surrounded by soldiers, while helicopters fly overhead.

WHEREVER WE MAY ROAM TOUR, PART I
29 October 1991–5 July 1992

The tour was buoyed by the incredible success of the *Black Album*, attracting audiences well beyond the circle of metal fans. Massive sums of money were now rolling in, and Metallica could put on outlandish shows with increasingly elaborate staging. This was when the infamous Snake Pit made its first appearance. A protected diamond-shaped area was set up in the middle of the stage for VIPs and fans with all-access passes. In the early days of the tour, the band settled for just 13 songs, but very soon Metallica shook up the set list and beat out more than 20 tracks in a riot of energy that put their bodies to the test. New songs were given more and more airtime during the show, which opened with the unstoppable "Enter Sandman", but now included "The Unforgiven", "Wherever I May Roam", "Sad But True" and "Holier Than You." The band hit the American roads at the end of October, before closing the pivotal year with a concert in Tokyo, Japan, on 31 December.

Even though 1991 ended with a live performance, the bootleg recording of which is still watched by legions of fans today, the Wherever We May Roam Tour was far from over. The *Black Album* continued to conquer the world and Metallica intended to benefit from its success in 1992. In January, the band gave four consecutive concerts in Los Angeles before moving on to Texas, Louisiana, Arkansas, Oklahoma, Tennessee, New Mexico, Colorado, Utah, Nevada and New York City. The musicians then attended the Grammys, where they won an award for "Enter Sandman". Between February and 5 July 1992, when the first part of the Wherever We May Roam Tour ended, Metallica travelled all over the United States and Canada and held a total of 75 gigs! They battled with a tough schedule, playing three concert dates and having just one night off.

The tour wrapped on 5 July at the Allentown Fairgrounds in Pennsylvania. But that's not the end of the story. The Four Horsemen's management and booking team had plenty more dates planned for 1992.

Right: James Hetfield at Cow Palace (San Francisco, California), on 15 May 1992.
Next page: Kirk Hammett in Rotterdam Ahoy (the Netherlands), 7 November 1992.

GUNS N' ROSES /METALLICA STADIUM TOUR

At that time, only the Guns could still compete with Metallica at the summit of global rock music. Axl, Slash and the band were at the height of their glory after the release of the diptych *Use Your Illusion I & II*, sustained by the unstoppable singles "Don't Cry" and "November Rain", which made the band the standard-bearer for largely mainstream hard rock. Why not bring the now-popular thrash superstars together with the hard rockers who had become the masters of overindulgence? The two bands toured together from 17 July 17 to 6 October. As a bonus, the bumper concert was supported by Faith No More, a band close to Metallica, some of whose members played with Cliff Burton.

Bill **GOULD**

'That was like working a shitty job. Axl had an army of lawyers and nobody was gonna do any direct confrontation with anybody else. [...] It was like working for a big corporation.'

RFK STADIUM:
CLASH OF THE TITANS
Washington, DC · 17 July 1992

The three bands met on 17 July at RFK Stadium in Washington DC to give a gig that promised to be memorable. For the occasion, Metallica reshuffled its set list and opened the show with an old favourite from *Ride the Lightning*, "Creeping Death", preferring to place the inevitable "Enter Sandman" in the encores, alongside "Nothing Else Matters". They probably chose this track to stand out from the hard rock served up by Guns N'Roses, and to hit fast and furious from the start with a very old-school thrash song. While the audience certainly got the show they wanted, and Metallica lived up to their reputation as live-show virtuosos, the offstage atmosphere between the two headliners was tense.

The sweet cocktail blended by their agents became more like an explosive Molotov. At the time, the Guns' sulphurous vocalist played the diva both on stage and behind the scenes and it didn't take long before his rather erratic behaviour towards the other bands began to grate. Bill Gould from Faith No More remembers: 'When you get into the big stadium rock shows, there's a lot of organization and a lot of people get in the way between the artist and the audience. There's security issues, there's all the shit... nothing really happens except this low level of unrest and grumbling. [...] On paper, this tour looked like the greatest opportunity in the world, to play in front of millions of people. But actually, it dragged on for like four or five months, and it was tough on our heads because we had been playing clubs before that.' While the fiasco seemed largely down to the singer of Guns N'Roses, the rivalry between the two headliners became more toxic as the tour went on, and relations between the bands broke down.

Jim Martin of Faith No More (left) and James Hetfield (right) during a concert at the Metrodrome in Minneapolis, Minnesota on 15 September 1992.

MONTREAL OLYMPIC STADIUM:
IF YOU PLAY WITH FIRE...
Montreal, Quebec · 8 August 1992

The logistical monster of a tour crossed New Jersey, Michigan, Indiana, New York and Pennsylvania. It filled the Giants Stadium in New Jersey before pushing on to Massachusetts, South Carolina and Minnesota and a final stop on 8 August in Montreal at the Olympic Stadium.

As usual, Metallica played to an excited crowd, attacking the 12th track of the set list, "Fade to Black", head on. In the middle of the song, one of the on-stage pyrotechnic effects exploded, hitting and seriously burning James Hetfield. Everything stopped, and James was immediately taken to get medical care.

The frontman suffered second- and third-degree burns all over his left arm and hand. If that wasn't enough to turn the evening into a nightmare, an unstable Axl Rose walked on stage, telling the shocked audience that the Guns wouldn't be playing either. Not because of the accident that had just happened, but quite simply because he had a sore throat and coudn't sing! Awkward...

The tour was put on hold while James got treatment for his injuries. The next seven shows of the Guns N'Roses/Metallica Stadium Tour were called off completely.

James Hetfield treats his burns backstage before a concert at Oakland stadium, California, on 21 August 1992.

Guns N'Roses,
arrogant glory

The Guns/Metallica tour didn't go quite as well as the promoters had hoped. Perhaps because they didn't realize they were throwing two bands with the same ambitions to be worldwide kings of rock into the same pit. The Guns were at the peak of their fame. Their first album, *Appetite for Destruction*, had sold 30 million copies and *Use Your Illusion* almost 35 million! Around the same time, the band was writing a song for the soundtrack of *Terminator 2: Judgment Day*, taking part in a tribute to Freddie Mercury and attending all the celebrity award ceremonies. Behind the scenes, the band was all about sex, drugs and rock'n'roll. Excessive in every way, Axl Rose was a caricature of hard rock, an explosive cocktail of glitter and extreme diva behaviour, which ended up being one of the causes of the band's slow agony, separations and failed reformations. Many early fans believed that the long-announced comeback album (*Chinese Democracy*) was set to be a damp squib.

PHOENIX INTERNATIONAL RACEWAY
Phoenix, Arizona · 25 August 1992

With injuries still smarting, James was determined to get back up on stage as quickly as possible, and the rock'n'roll circus thundered back into town on 25 August in Phoenix, Arizona. Just like when he broke his wrist six years earlier, James gave the role of rhythm guitarist to his old friend and roadie John Marshall, and the frontman stuck to singing for the remainder of the tour. He was seen wearing a thick bandage from elbow to wrist, his hands free to express his emotions like never before! A glimpse of these shows is available in the documentary

A Year and a Half in the Life of Metallica, which features the live performance of "Nothing Else Matters" at a gig in Avondale.

More dates followed in New Mexico, Louisiana, Georgia, Florida, Texas, South Carolina, Massachusetts, Canada, Minnesota, Missouri, Colorado and California, with the gruelling tour coming to an end in Washington State on 6 October. By the time the tour wrapped, the two bands had fallen out completely.

WHEREVER WE MAY ROAM TOUR II AND III

While the band was touring on the roads of America with the Guns and Faith No More, the *Black Album* was racking up huge sales on the other side of the Atlantic, winning over a growing number of fans throughout Europe. Boosted by the good news, the band and its entourage got ready for a series of dates for the endless Wherever We May Roam Tour and Metallica was once again on its way to the Old Continent.

WHEREVER WE MAY ROAM TOUR, PART II
22 October 1992–8 May 1993

In an approach that had paid dividends in the past, Metallica got back to its roots, once again offering a balanced live performance that included old songs and fan favourites from the latest album. The concerts opened again with "Enter Sandman" and the tracks on ...*And Justice for All* were featured in a mid-set medley, while the dark ballad "Nothing Else Matters" logically found its place in the second half of the gig after a long guitar solo.

This same set was played (almost exactly) from 22 October at concerts in Ghent, Belgium, London (at the legendary Wembley Stadium), Glasgow, Newcastle, Dublin, Sheffield, Manchester, Birmingham, Rotterdam and, finally at Bercy arena in Paris on 10 November 1992. After their roaring success with the French crowd, the Four Horsemen pushed on to Spain, Italy, Switzerland, Austria, Germany (where they performed ten concerts!), the Netherlands, Denmark, Sweden, Norway and Finland. At every gig, the *Black-Album*-loving audience went into a trance. When it was all over, the weary musicians finally boarded a plane for the United States to take a few weeks of rest after a frenetic 1992.

Opposite: Jason Newsted at the NEC Arena in Birmingham, UK on 4 November 1992.
Above: James Hetfield at the same time, on the other side of the stage.

A FIRST AT BERCY!
Paris, France · 10 November 1992

Metallica took to the stage at the Palais Omnisports de Paris-Bercy for the first time this year, and the venue was on fire. When the last chords of the first track, "Enter Sandman", sounded, the Four Horsemen had already won over the crowd. James, Kirk and Jason were perched on a triangular stage whose tip cut through the audience like the bow of a gigantic ship. Lars was perched high up as usual, at the top of some steps leading to another stage. The other members of the band paraded up and down the steps during the performance.

A fiery James Hetfield whipped up the Parisian crowd, who replied in unison with a thunder of wild howls. "Creeping Death" got going with its diabolical riff, and the French crowd sang all the lyrics, even taking over from James in some of the verses. The audience was enchanted by their idols and James gushed to his fans during the many breaks. After an hour and 45 minutes, the band received an extended standing ovation from the fans at Bercy, who chanted 'Metallica' at the tops of their voices. The band left the stage and the screaming spectators' applause lasted more than five minutes, before Kirk Hammett began playing the "Nothing Else Matters" arpeggio, seated on the steps of the stage in the glow of simple white spotlight. The French crowd sang the entire song in perfect unison. The atmosphere was electric.

Metallica stayed for an encore of six songs, and the gig went on for over two and a half hours!

Opposite: Lars, the devil incarnate!
Right: Kirk Hammett, deep in concentration during one of his legendary solos!

FROM WHEREVER WE MAY ROAM, PART III...
22 January–8 May 199

With itchy feet and driven by the planetary success of the *Black Album*, Metallica got back to touring on 22 January 1993 for a new American extravaganza. They performed 26 gigs in the United States, Canada and Mexico, through to the beginning of March: an average of one show every two days! And since nothing could stop the huge Wherever We May Roam Tour, a series of dates in the Pacific and South America was also scheduled. In total, the tour's international leg included 30 gigs in Hawaii, Japan, New Zealand, Australia, Indonesia, Singapore, Thailand, the Philippines, Brazil, Chile and finally Argentina.

...TO NOWHERE ELSE TO ROAM
19 May–30 June 1993

Taking a step back from the band's journey, which had started more than two years previously, by 1993 Metallica had clearly conquered the world. They had played gigs in Europe, the Southern Hemisphere, Asia and throughout North and South America, so where did they go from here? Back on the road.

By this time, public demand for the band was insatiable, and that explains the ironic name for the tour. Metallica headed back to Europe, returning to Germany, the Czech Republic, Denmark, Sweden, Finland, England, Slovakia, Hungary, the Netherlands, France, Portugal, Spain, Switzerland, Italy, Turkey, Austria, Greece, Israel and Belgium, playing one last gig on 4 July 1993 at the Rock Werchter Festival alongside Lenny Kravitz, Neil Young, Sonic Youth and many others.

By the early summer of 1993, Metallica had proven that they could reach well beyond the world of metal, with the band scheduled to appear at more "mainstream" festivals. Metallica was at the top of its musical game.

On 12 June 1993, James and the rest of his band light up the stage at the Feijenoord stadium in Rotterdam (the Netherlands).

Estadio Palestra Italia (Brazil)
2 May 1993

Like many of the concerts on this Southern Hemisphere tour, and more particularly the live shows in South America, Metallica's show brought together all the flammable ingredients for a successful live rock performance: a huge stadium (most South American football stadiums are enormous), a devoted crowd committed to the cause of rock and metal (many bands in the same genre have built up a solid fanbase throughout the continent), a full-on concert experience (as global stars visit on a much rarer basis, they attract a massive crowd) and gargantuan staging. On this part of the tour, the band brought a colossal metal structure to support the stage. They also erected giant screens on each side so that the audience could enjoy the concert even if they were a long way back. During the introduction, the entire stadium was plunged into darkness, then projected images flooded onto the two huge screens. The fans went crazy. And when the first notes of "Enter Sandman" rang out, the crowd (perhaps 80,000, perhaps 100,000) morphed into a raging, undulating mass of yelling and raised arms. Just like in Paris, the musicians heard the crowd singing the verses of the songs in unison, then the noise shifted to shrieks between each track. Also like in Paris, the thunderous show lasted two and a half hours and left the entire stadium enthralled.

DISC #1

1. Enter Sandman
2. Creeping Death
3. Harvester of Sorrow
4. Welcome Home (Sanitarium)
5. Sad But True
6. Of Wolf and Man
7. The Unforgiven
8. Justice Medley
9. Eye of The Beholder
10. Blackened
11. The Frayed Ends of Sanity
12. ...And Justice For All
13. Blackened
14. Solos

DISC #2

1. Through the Never
2. For Whom the Bell Tolls
3. Fade to Black
4. Master of Puppets
5. Seek and Destroy
6. Whiplash

DISC #3

1. Nothing Else Matters
2. Wherever I May Roam
3. Am I Evil?
4. Last Caress
5. One
6. So What?
7. The Four Horsemen
8. Motorbreath
9. Stone Cold Crazy

VHS #1

1. The Ecstasy of Gold
2. Enter Sandman
3. Creeping Death
4. Harvester of Sorrow
5. Welcome Home (Sanitarium)
6. Sad But True
7. Wherever I May Roam
8. Solos
9. Through the Never
10. The Unforgiven
11. Justice Medley :
    - Eye of The Beholder
    - Blackened
    - The Frayed Ends of Sanity
    - ...And Justice For All
12. Guitar Solo
13. Drum Solo

VHS #2

1. The Four Horsemen
2. For Whom the Bell Tolls
3. Fade to Black
4. Whiplash
5. Master of Puppets
6. Seek and Destroy
7. One
8. Last Caress
9. Am I Evil?
10. Battery
11. Stone Cold Crazy

VHS #3

1. The Ecstasy of Gold / Blackened
2. For Whom the Bell Tolls
3. Welcome Home (Sanitarium)
4. Harvester of Sorrow
5. The Four Horsemen
6. The Thing That Should Not Be
7. Solos
8. Master of Puppets
9. Fade to Black
10. Seek and Destroy
11. ...And Justice For All
12. One
13. Creeping Death
14. Guitar Solo
15. Battery
16. The Frayed Ends of Sanity
17. Last Caress / Am I Evil?
18. Whiplash
19. Breadfan

Live Sh*t: Binge & Purge,
the iconic box set

In a rare twist of fate, Metallica managed to take a real break from the stage for several months in a row (from July 1993 to May 1994) for the first time in many years. Obviously, the tour marathon that followed the release of the *Black Album* put a physical strain on the band, and as we will see later, this had an impact on their music. But Lars and James soon got itchy feet once the excitement of the tour had died down and there were no immediate plans to get back out on the road. So, they decided to embark on a massive series of live recordings. The production work was immense: listening, sorting and mixing took many months, but the band eventually produced its first live album. On 29 November 1993, a huge collection of three CDs and three video cassettes was released, entitled *Live Shit: Binge and Purge*.

The album was sold as a cardboard container designed to look like a typical tour equipment transportation box, which reflected the Metallica of this period. Although it was criticized for being too expensive at $85, the huge quantity of sound and video recordings it contained made it a cult object that every fan must own.

The band sold 600,000 copies of the must-have box set, proving that despite their temporary absence from the stage, the band was still very much at the forefront of people's minds. Releasing this live album allowed the band to put this incredible period after the *Black Album* behind them, as Lars explained at the time: 'I think it's turned into a great way of getting the last three and a half years out

of our systems. Now the slate really is completely clean. We wrote the album, made the album, toured the album and here's the documentation of the album's music on the road. Now we can take our nine months or whatever off and start with a clean slate. Everything about this tour is gone. It will enable us to completely let go of everything from the last few years, and when we begin to approach the next album we can do so without any lingering, leftover baggage.' And for once, the band kept its promises. Fans didn't see Metallica again until the following spring when they began the new tour in 1994: Shit Hits the Sheds, the first date of which took place on 30 May in Buffalo, New York.

SHIT HITS THE SHEDS TOUR
30 May–21 August 1994

True to form, Metallica launched into one of its characteristic mammoth road trips along the familiar highways of the United States. Two groups went with James and his band: Danzig and Suicidal Tendencies. They brought a brand of metal with a funk-rap flavour, a genre on the rise. The tour made stops in New Jersey, Pennsylvania, Vermont, Massachusetts, New Hampshire, Ohio, Michigan, Iowa, Wisconsin, Missouri, Indiana, Illinois, Washington, Oregon, California, Arizona, Utah, Nevada, New Mexico, Colorado, Texas and Oklahoma.

The band gave a total of 51 concerts in under three months, with a grand finale at Bicentennial Park in Miami, Florida on 21 August 1994. The highlight of the long American tour was that Metallica got to meet a certain Robert Trujillo, who was playing with their support band, Suicidal Tendencies. The bassist got a chance to display his musical talents to the biggest metal band in the world and his endearing character appealed to Lars and James. It wouldn't be long before their paths crossed again...

Lars **ULRICH**

'It's our first attempt at a live package, and it's definitely the right time in our career to do this. It's also the right time for us to take a step away from everything for however long.'

The latest road trip of the United States in the summer of 1994 wrapped up the massive promotion for the global phenomenon that was the *Black Album*. It was a turning point in the band's career, attracting an international mainstream audience to Metallica. But as always, far from resting on their hard-earned laurels, James, Lars, Kirk and Jason were already thinking about what came next. A few months later, on 30 October 1994, the musicians got back into the studio to start writing their next album. And the process of creating *Load* began. Recordings got under way in February of the following year, still under the stewardship of producer Bob Rock, who had done such a great job on the *Black Album* sound.

A SUPERSONIC JET AT CRUISING ALTITUDE

When the release date of the successor to the *Black Album* was announced, fans around the world were waiting with bated breath. Would the new album live up to its phenomenal predecessor? Would the band return to its thrash roots? Would they play uptempo songs again? What would they do on stage?

Admittedly, Metallica had reached an unprecedented status on the world stage with its latest tours. At the time, it was the only thrash-era band to have performed so many times in all four corners of the planet. What more was there for Metallica to do?

With Poor Touring Me, Poor Re-Touring Me, then The Garage Remains the Same and Blitzkrieg '97, the upcoming tours celebrated past successes while attracting an even wider audience, drawn to the band after their legendary festival performances throughout the world. The story was far from over!

A GLORIOUS RETURN

Metallica proved that it was still going strong, opening its music to mainstream audiences. The band began their upcoming promotional tour at the Lollapalooza festival. Then, as usual, the band played an ultra-marathon consisting of two huge tours around Europe and the United States.

LOLLAPALOOZA FESTIVAL
Irvine, California · 4 August 1996

The bill for this festival not only lists metal or heavy metal bands. Since 1991, Lollapalooza has welcomed indie performers of all kinds, whether they specialize in rock, rap or indie rock, grunge or industrial music. During the 1996 festival, Metallica found itself alongside Soundgarden, the Ramones, Melvins and Rancid, to name just a few of the most famous. The festival began on 27 June 1996 in Kansas City and continued throughout the month of July, racking up a total of 23 gigs!

Finally, after more than a month on tour, the festival arrived in Irvine, California.

On this day, a large stage was set up in an amphitheatre, and the scheduled bands performed one after the other. Metallica was obviously the headliner. As always, the band kicked off hard. They opened the show with a very basic (but effective) cover of Anti-Nowhere League's "So What", which they released later (alongside others) on

the *Garage Inc.* album. The audience was thrilled to see their heroes again and went wild right from the first bars. During the first third of the song (which the band seemed to use as a line check), they stopped playing and James shrieked at the crowd: 'SO FUCKING WHAT?!' Delighted, the mass of bodies howled back and the track got going again. The fans were safe in the knowledge that even though Metallica had stopped making so many records, the on-stage machine was still well oiled and ready for action. The set list was a series of classics that had won over fans at countless gigs: "Creeping Death", "Sad But True", "Whiplash", "Fade to Black", and many more.

The new edge to the band was only revealed during the ninth track, with "Until It Sleeps". The first chords rang out in an intimate, dusky atmosphere tinged with blue. Lars played alongside Jason's bass line in a midtempo rhythm; he was almost restrained and gave cold wave vibes. James stood in his favourite position while singing the track but refrained from shrieking or howling at the crowd. His voice was clear and calm, and the new Metallica introduced itself to the Californian audience. When the chorus was unleashed, heavy chords and melodic precision replaced stampedes and thrash energy. The band was now playing a style of heavy rock that alternated crisp guitar arpeggios and magisterial choruses, with Jason on backing vocals to support James. It created a new reaction from the crowd. They were observant, static, attentive. Far removed from the long-haired hordes that used to headbang with James!

On 4 August 1996 at the Lollapalooza festival in Irvine, Kirk Hammett and his three companions show off their short hair.

So What
Creeping Death
Sad But True
Ain't My Bitch
Whiplash
Fade to Black
King Nothing
One
Until It Sleeps
For Whom the Bell Tolls
Wherever I May Roam
Nothing Else Matters
Enter Sandman
Last Caress
Master of Puppets

But there was no way that Metallica would give their fans any real respite. They launched into "For Whom the Bell Tolls" and "Wherever I May Roam", followed by the two classics: "Nothing Else Matters" and "Enter Sandman" to get the crowds pumping again. There's no doubt about it: Metallica was back. With shorter hair, yes, but fitter than ever and aching to continue their musical dominance. The band members still had their signature viciousness, and the heaviest tracks were the ones they seemed to enjoy most. On this tour, they played "Sad But True" in a slower style, which gave the main riff even greater power. And the stage performance by James during this part echoed

that power; he shook his head until his neck almost broke! Lars's face was split into a carnivorous, almost vicious smile as he pounded his hi-hat.

The gig ended in a deluge of noise and double bass drum as the band launched into a cover of the famous "Overkill" by Motörhead. The fans were ecstatic to see the band's leader, Lemmy, join Metallica on stage to bring their live performance comeback to a magnificent climax. Lollapalooza 1996 was over, and Metallica was already getting ready for their next promotional tour for the new album, which began right after this furious warm-up in the USA.

Next page: Jason, James and Kirk rehearsing for the 1996 MTV Video Music Awards.

A new era, a new look

A few weeks before their new album was officially released, the band did a series of press interviews. Right from the outset, journalists and fans noticed that the musicians had cut their hair and changed out of their typical metal clothing. The foursome now had cropped locks, which at the time was unheard of in metal circles! Later, some said this was when the band turned its back on the "real metal" that had made them famous.

And that's not all. During media interviews, James and the others were much more particular than ever before about wardrobe choices. In the photos for the album, taken by fashion photographer Anton Corbijn, there was a clear shift in style: a 1930s-style floppy hat for Kirk, striped trousers and braces for James, mascara and slicked back hair for Lars. The band looked completely different and as they entered the second half of the 90s; the band was beginning a new chapter.

Lars
ULRICH

'We're a lot more respectful. We have some fun with each other but the most important thing fo us is to go on stage and play good and connect and do our thing, and right now we're doing that probably the best we've ever done.'

WINNING BACK EUROPE
6 September–27 November 1996

In September, after a few more shows in the United States (some of which were televised to promote the new album), Metallica flew to Europe. Their schedule was packed; they had been booked for a marathon tour that only they could handle. This new show was called Poor Touring Me, in reference to the track "Poor Twisted Me" that appears on *Load*. The band played more than 120 concerts in 19 different countries, and the marathon began on 6 September in Vienna, Austria. The standard set list based on their performance at Lollapalooza gave pride of place to the band's old songs, while bringing a taste of the new album.

The band delivered understated 90s style and the tour's pared-down staging followed suit. Gone were the giant superstructures that recalled their album cover artwork. For this tour, the band's first priority was to get close to its fans. The stage was built with a huge apron that extended right into the crowd, bringing the musicians nose to nose with the rest of the Metallica family. On many of the dates, the Metallica boys arrived on stage with no introduction and before the house lights had been switched off. This happened when the Four Horsemen stopped off in Paris on 15 September 1996 for two consecutive sold-out concerts...

So What
Creeping Death
Sad But True
Ain't My Bitch
Whiplash
Bleeding Me
King Nothing
One
Wasting My Hate
Bass and guitar solos
Nothing Else Matters
Until It Sleeps
For Whom the Bell Tolls
Wherever I May Roam
Fade to Black
Kill/Ride Medley

The Shortest Straw
Master of Puppets
Enter Sandman
Last Caress
Breadfan
Motorbreath

Palais omnisports de Bercy, Paris
25 September 1996

Once Corrosion of Conformity had finished their opener, the Bercy speakers churned out hard rock and metal to fill the void. The packed venue was bathed in light. The band members were almost nonchalant as they wandered up the steps towards the stage. A relaxed James greeted the fans and scratched out a few riffs while the musicians each took a position at the edge of the stage.

As with the Lollapalooza Tour, Metallica began its set with the effective "So What", casually played with the house lights still up, as if it were just another track for the soundcheck. This raw, almost punk kick-off contrasts sharply with the elaborate staging and spectacle of previous tours. Times had changed, grunge had made its mark, and Metallica knew the score. It was a statement of intent that fitted perfectly with the raw and almost basic efficiency of *Load*. The show proper didn't really begin until the first chords of "Creeping Death" burst ferociously from the speakers.

The arena was dark, and coloured projector beams singled out each player. The four musicians occupied the entire stage, enjoying the attention of their fans. James, Kirk and Jason constantly switched positions, roaming freely from one end to the other. Several microphones were set up around the stage, so James and Jason, on backing vocals, could sing from wherever they happened to be. The immense, circus-like spectacle so typical of 80s metal had yielded to a minimalist show that focused on raw effectiveness and proximity to the crowd.

The only concession to the spectacular metal tradition was the pyrotechnic effects that exploded when the verse of "Creeping Death" began. The hysteria peaked when this first track ended, with the crowd at Bercy chanting the band's name. James replied: 'Has Paris missed Metallica? You are fucking crazy guys, Metallica missed you too! We're here to play some heavy metal! It's very heavy! Are you ready?' Unsurprisingly, the sea of Parisians was delighted when the band launched into a colossal version of "Sad But True". Then came the most powerful hits ("Whiplash", "One" and so on), but Metallica also performed the new tracks from *Load*: "Ain't My Bitch", "Bleeding Me", "King Nothing", "Wasting My Hate", "Until It Sleeps". Each musician had his own white followspot, and because they were all constantly moving around, the beams crisscrossed each other in a frenzy of light. The screaming fans couldn't get enough and the mosh pit was a forest of arms.

Metallica had returned to Europe on a wave of success and even managed to satisfy early fans with a formidable medley intelligently placed in the middle of the set compiling excerpts from "Ride the Lightning", "No Remorse", "Hit the Lights", "The Four Horsemen", "Seek & Destroy" and "Fight Fire With Fire."

This hugely popular concert was typical of the entire tour. Metallica were at the top of their game, and the musicians had polished the new tracks to perfection without losing sight of their thrash roots. On 27 November, the band finished its mammoth European tour. Next step: the United States.

GREAT WESTERN FORUM

Los Angeles, California
21 December 1996

Back from the Old Continent, the band took a short rest before getting back out onto the familiar roads of the United States. On 19 December 1996, Metallica began a very long journey. They started at Fresno's Selland Arena in their beloved California, then gave a show in Los Angeles two days later, which set the tone for all the other gigs on this American tour.

The room was bathed in light as the band members appeared from the wings to a deafening roar. Jason walked towards the audience and tapped one of the staff members on the shoulder as if they were wishing each other good luck. The crowd shrieked in response and James jogged over to the pit between the crowd and the stage, high-fiving the excited fans in the front row. Unlike on previous tours when the band made a dramatic entrance after a long introduction, Metallica now got going jam-style, with "The Memory Remains", as if this were the last soundcheck before the gig proper.

James and the others stopped after just a few bars. Lars stood up behind his drum kit and the crowd begged for more… 'Oh yeah? Oh yeah?' said James into the microphone, and the mass of fans went wild before the band launched into a punk-rock-like "Last Caress" with youthful spontaneity. The show didn't get into full swing until the opening bars of "Creeping Death". The main lights were switched off, only the footlights remained. That evening, the band gave their all for over two hours, ending in double-pedal debauchery with a cover of "Overkill", Motörhead's biker hit.

Dripping with sweat after a wild yet beautifully choreographed show, James and Lars took off their shirts. Delighted, the band thanked the audience and left the stage.

Lars ULRICH

'We're in better shape than we've ever been in before. We're definitely having our fun, but overall we're probably partying less than we did when we played in America before. I'm in much better shape than I was in '92. I'm running, doing my five or six miles. Aerobically and physically I'm in much better shape than I've ever been in before. I can feel that it's not much of a struggle. I can remember nights on the 92 tour where I'd struggle to get through the last hour but I don't feel that any more.'

A FINALE AT EDMONTON COLISEUM
Alberta, Canada · 28 May 1997

Metallica reunited with their fans, touring almost the entire United States until 28 May. They played a total of 86 concerts – one every other day – for almost six months.

The band performed the last date on its massive tour to a packed stadium full of screaming Canadian admirers. The enormous central stage stood in the middle of the mosh pit and the band started the gig under the harsh white spotlights with an unbridled version of "So What".

After a gruelling series of gigs in Europe and throughout the United States, the band was tighter than ever. Lars even indulged in a few pranks, standing up behind his drums to scan the audience, hand above his eyes, like a sailor peering into the distance. The rock machine was totally relaxed, and played an impeccable set list, getting the crowd involved on a few songs and inviting the members of Corrosion of Conformity on stage to celebrate the end of the joint tour.

While sobriety seemed to be the order of the day in terms of musical composition and lifestyle, the members of Metallica still indulged in a little fantasy when it came to the staging they set up every night before their gigs. At the end of the show, James pretended he had been hit by a pyrotechnic effect and left the stage. A few seconds later,

a stuntman dressed in a fire suit appeared. The human torch collapsed, feigning agony, while a group of rescuers rushed towards him... The prank was supposed to attract the fans' attention, because it was reminiscent of the accident James had a few years earlier. But they were left feeling disconcerted, as Lars remembers: 'I gotta tell you, even with press and the internet I'm pretty amazed... the other day we were signing autographs and these girls said, "Tell your pyro guys we hope they're OK." About 75 per cent of the people I talked to believed it's real. They're saying, "I can't believe you kept playing with a guy running around on stage on fire!"'

Whatever, James and Lars were delighted with what they accomplished, and went on setting up more and more pranks. This final concert came to an end to rapturous applause, and James lapped up the glory: 'We had some fun baby!' he shouted into the microphone before the whole band came out to acknowledge their devoted fans. Kirk and Lars hugged each other and James revelled in the crowd's adoration. Darkness fell on the Edmonton Coliseum and on this last Poor Touring Me concert in North America. And that was a wrap.

A FEAST OF FESTIVALS

After releasing *Load* and proving that Metallica was alive and kicking, the band took on a new challenge: *Blitzkrieg '97*. Three consecutive concerts in three countries at three different music festivals. The band showed once again how it had entered the pop world through the metal door, reaching a wide audience who saw Metallica as a band of music legends, not just thrashers. This reputation set the band apart and gave them an in to a gigantic show in a parking lot in Philadelphia the following November. It was 1997, and Metallica was the stuff of legends.

1, 2, 3... READING FESTIVAL
Reading, England · 24 August 1997

Three days, three festivals. Blitzkrieg '97 will undoubtedly remain the smallest tour ever given by a major metal band. After the Pukkelpop Festival in Belgium on 22 August and Blindman's Ball in Germany on 23 August, Metallica wrapped up with the world-famous Reading Festival in England. The band was scheduled to appear on the main stage on the last day of the ultimate 90s rock event. Metallica had the responsiblity of closing three days of non-stop music featuring bands as varied as Suede, The Manic Street Preachers, Dinosaur Jr., Eels, The Cardigans, The Jon Spencer Blues Explosion, Dog Eat Dog, Stereolab, The Verve, Cake, Death in Vegas and The Orb, to name just a few.

Unsurprisingly, the stage was huge and flanked by two giant screens. On this occasion, Metallica set aside their usual stage quirks and played in a more conventional formation, Lars sat at the back of the stage and the three others covered the entire width at the front.
Obviously eagerly awaited, the Four Horsemen began their set by pounding out the traditional "So What", to an electric audience that had already enjoyed three days of music. It was a huge sound. Powerful and precise.
Unlike the set list from the previous tour, Metallica got a kick out of running straight into a frenetic shortened version of "Master of Puppets", probably in an effort to show the rock and pop audience

So What
Master Of Puppets
King Nothing
Sad But True
Fuel
Hero Of The Day
Ain't My Bitch
One
Until It Sleeps
For Whom The Bell Tolls
Wherever I May Roam
Nothing Else Matters
Enter Sandman
_____
Stone Cold Crazy
Creeping Death
Battery
Last Caress
Motorbreath

what real thrash was all about. And it worked! The crowd was in ecstasy, singing along to all the choruses in the throbbing track. A giant mass of bodies jumped as one in front of the stage. James even let the audience sing certain parts of the track in his place. And when the heavy riffs in the vicious bass line resonated during the first bars of "King Nothing" (from the latest album), the crowd responded with warlike chanting. The flawless show reflected the goal Metallica set for itself when it released *Load*: to be an all-terrain band that appealed to hordes of thrashers and mainstream audiences at the world's major festivals. The unforgettable gig lasted almost an hour and a half. The crowd was wild and stretched back as far as the eye could see.

Jason Newsted is proud to wear a Metallica T-shirt at the 1997 Reading Festival

THE MILLION DECIBEL MARCH
Philadelphia, Pennsylvania
11 November 1997

Metallica had already toured Europe, the American continent, played several major festivals and was preparing to release a new album. It was called *Reload* and contained a set of tracks from the recording sessions made for the previous album. At the height of its popularity, the foursome was getting ready to hit the road again to promote the new record, but kept one important event in mind. They wanted to give a concert to honour their American fans. Humbly titled The Million Decibels March, the event was to take place in Philadelphia... in a huge parking lot!

Metallica thought big, installing a gigantic stage and a monstrous sound system smack bang in the middle of a residential area. The project inevitably worried the local population and those in charge. City councillor James Kenney said: 'On the face of it, I think it would be a big mistake. Once again, you're going to have problems with crowds in a residential area. You'll have noise and traffic congestion... If the heavy-metal rock band wants to hold a concert here, why not hold it inside the CoreStates Spectrum? And if you're putting all these Beavis and Buttheads in the parking lot, where are you going to park the cars?'

James responded to the outcry with a press release to explain what the group wanted to achieve: 'We asked our fans to find us a place to play, and they came through. And now on November 11 we're going to blow them away. There's no better place to play millions of decibels than the Hard-CoreStates arena.'

The band was cleared to play. Right at sunset, the Four Horsemen climbed the steps up to the immense stage surrounded by scaffolding. The audience howled. The giant parking lot was packed, smoke bombs creating the look of a war zone as Lars marched towards his drum kit. The band had a new set list for the occasion and opened with "Helpless" and its typically thrash riff. "The Four Horsemen", "Of Wolf and Man" and "The Thing That Should Not Be" were up next. Old tracks were sandwiched between new, and the crowd was a cacophony of screaming between each one.

After the concert, a reporter from the *Philadelphia Inquirer* wrote: 'It was part burlesque show, part rugby match, and hearing-loss loud. The band was profane on stage and charming before the show. Police pronounced the fans better behaved than a Philadelphia Eagles crowd. And neighbors who feared the worst from the self-styled Loudest Band in the World complained more about the sound from the news choppers circling overhead.' A triumph.

Load, Reload :
the beginning of the end?

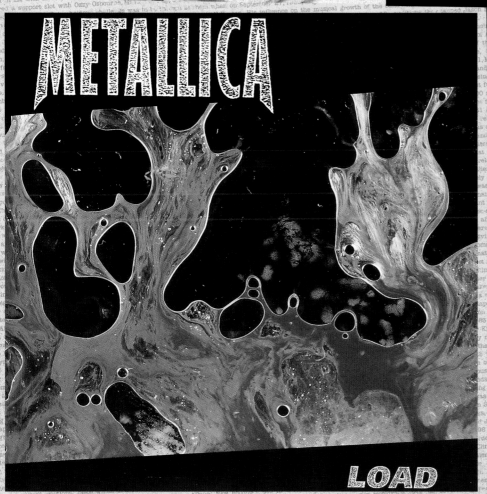

While the hardest-core fans see the *Black Album* as an unacceptable musical turning point, the consecutive release of the *Load* and *Reload* declared Metallica's thrash metal origins dead and buried. Admittedly, the *Black Album* was so incredibly successful that fans were hungry for the band to release a new record.

Recorded once again under the stewardship of producer Bob Rock, the diptych disappointed a very large number of fans, from diehard metalheads to those who had succumbed to the magic of "Nothing Else Matters". For many, there just wasn't enough new material. Worn-out riffs, lazy compositions, hackneyed melodies and rebellious heavy rock, the press at the time had a field day and few journalists and fans ran to the band's defence. Where the band had perfectly succeeded in its transformation between a cold and complex *...And Justice for All* and a hit-packed and magnificently produced *Black Album*, *Load/Reload* gets stuck in throats, gracelessly entangled in a plump and cramped production whose vision of blues borders on FM. A tough pill to swallow.

THE NEXT (OBVIOUS) STEP: RELOAD

Metallica fans were surprised to see a new album drop so soon after *Load*. They had got used to the band taking the album on long world tours before getting back down to creating new music again. What they didn't know was that the two albums in the *Load* era were in fact recorded during the same studio session. Later, James explained that *Load* and *Reload* were intended to be released as one album, but in the end, they decided to release them separately in quick succession. *Reload* came out on 18 November 1997 and its promotional tour began on 2 April of the following year. It lasted until 13 September.

RETURN TO ASIA: OLYMPIC GYMNASTICS ARENA

Seoul, South Korea · 24 April 1998

Although the band toured with the *Black Album* all over Asia and Oceania, the two continents didn't feature on the *Load* tour. That meant the release of *Reload* was a perfect opportunity to reconnect with Asian and Australian fans during the first leg. James and his bandmates had never travelled so extensively around this part of the world. Taking in Australia, New Zealand, South Korea and Japan, Metallica performed 22 concerts between 2 April and 8 May.

So What
Master of Puppets
King Nothing
Ain't My Bitch
Sad But True
Fuel
The Memory Remains
Bleeding Me
Bass and guitar solos
Nothing Else Matters
Until It Sleeps
For Whom the Bell Tolls
Wherever I May Roam
One
Kill / Ride Medley

Low Man's Lyric
The Four Horsemen
Motorbreath
Creeping Death
Enter Sandman
Battery

The band didn't do things by halves on their Asian tour. After wrapping the Japanese tour at a venue that also contained an Olympic-sized pool, the 24 April show in South Korea took place in a cavernous sports hall and the organizers had set up thousands of plastic chairs in neat little rows for the mosh pit. The band wondered if its fans were going to sit quietly, and if this was going to be a dull concert. But once the first song, "So What", was over, all the Metallica fan family were up on their chairs, waving their arms and singing along to "Master of Puppets". Every now and then, James stopped singing to listen.

Following on from the *Load* promotional tour, Metallica played an almost identical set list, merging "King Nothing" into "Sad But True" and playing "Fuel" (from *Reload*) in fifth position. And while *Reload* received mixed reviews when it was released, these Asian audiences really let loose to the track, certainly one of the strongest on the record.

The band played 20 songs, as usual mixing hits from the past (like the famous mid-concert thrash medley) and power ballad ("Nothing Else Matters") before wiping out the audience with the formidable "Battery". The tour ended on 8 May 1998 in Japan and the band headed back to the United States to perform the biggest chunk of the Poor Retouring Me extravaganza, which took them across their native country throughout the summer through to early autumn.

STONE RIDGE
Washington, DC · 28 June 1998

The band was riding on a wave of popularity that seemed unstoppable, despite their many early fans making no bones about their hatred of the current record. But the musicians were still playing to sold-out crowds every night, in part because their performances were a subtle blend of the strongest tracks from their entire back catalogue, rather than simply a live version of their latest album. The sound was huge and the band were perfectly relaxed on stage; they seemed to have reached a certain level of maturity. Admittedly, with their relentless gig schedule, Metallica had built up on-stage experience that is almost unprecedented in the history of rock and metal. The well-oiled Metallica machine hit the roads of the United States again on 24 June 1998, heading into a scorching summer that wouldn't be over until 13 September. Metallica performed 39 gigs across the United States.

The band were top of the bill for most of the tour, coming on after two support acts: Days of the New and Jerry Cantrell, the founder of Alice in Chains, who was pursuing a solo career at the time. The crowd had already reached fever pitch when the last bars of "The Ecstasy of Gold", by Ennio Morricone, rang out.

On the evening of 28 June at Stone Ridge, Metallica decided to launch headlong into their live show with "Helpless". James whipped up the audience with everything he had. The stage was bathed in a fiery orange glow, recalling the colours of the *Reload* album cover. Sharper than ever, Lars and his double pedal hammered the audience's eardrums, while Kirk went wild on a masterful solo. When the end finally came, James raged with a 'Hail! Hail! Hail!' in time with the beat. The band was fully flexed and ready for action. Next came the unstoppable "Master of Puppets" which – as usual – stirred up the crowd. Lars was on fire, he sprang from behind his kit and riled up the fans, the musical metal machine in full control at the tips of his drumsticks.

After the traditional acoustic part of the concert, which saw Metallica perform "Low Man's Lyric", "The Four Horsemen" and "Motorbreath", the band indulged the audience with three of its biggest hits: "Sad But True", "Enter Sandman" and "Creeping Death". With fans on their knees, Metallica left the stage after an almost two-hour concert.

Jerry Cantrell, founder of Alice in Chains, solos to open for Metallica on part of the tour.

A SHOW OF FORCE
AT GIANTS STADIUM

East Rutherford, New Jersey · 17 July 1998

On 17 July 1998, Metallica performed a memorable gig at Giants Stadium in New Jersey. The band was filling stadiums at the time, and this show was no different. With a capacity of more than 80,000 spectators, this stadium was one of the largest in the United States during the late 90s. The band took to the stage and clocked the human tide that had flowed into the arena during its famous introduction, which suggested Metallica had returned to its roots. Giving a hint of the direction for the next album, Metallica began this concert with an incredibly impressive cover entitled "Breadfan", and continued with the now traditional "Master of Puppets".

With understated scenery, a black stage and rather traditional lighting effects, Metallica was no longer looking for artificial performance enhancers. The music spoke for itself. However, James was sometimes surprised not to hear the crowd chanting the choruses. And while the band had booked three dates outside the contiguous United States to close this tour (Hawaii, Mexico and Anchorage), they were postponed indefinitely to make way for a new chapter in the band's history.

Below: The Four Horsemen at the 1999 Billboard Music Awards.
They win two trophies.
Next page: James and Kirk at the Roseland Ballroom
(New York), 24 November 1998.

GARAGE INC.
EVERYONE GETS THEIR KICKS

In September, the band rushed back to the studio to record a new album. *Garage Inc.* was released on 24 November and Metallica gave several concerts before embarking on the major promotional tour the following spring. The tour began in Latin America and continued to Europe for a series of concerts called The Garage Remains the Same between 30 April and 24 July. The high point of the tour took place on 23 May in the Netherlands, at what was at the time the largest metal festival in Europe, Dynamo Open Air.

A MEETING OF METALS
AT DYNAMO OPEN AIR

Eindhoven, the Netherlands · 23 May 1999

At the time, Dynamo was considered by all European metal fans as the biggest festival of its kind. Since the band's thrash beginnings, the metal scene had completely transformed. Thrash had been taken over by death and black metal, Metallica had spawned countless bands (including Pantera and Sepultura), gothic music had emerged, and the Four Horsemen's heavy rock style was struggling to convince diehards of the genre. But the festival programming team put Metallica on the bill alongside 72 other groups for three days of concerts, presenting them as the special event to close the festival.

Proving wrong those who thought the band had turned its back on "real metal" with *Load* and *Reload*, Metallica was a huge success and the crowd happily sang along to every word of "Master of Puppets".

The sun set on the vast Eindhoven landscape with the band in full swing. Kirk and the others were dripping with sweat as they raced around the stage. This was a battle of pure metal, their only weapon an arsenal of enormous hits. The crowd was hungry for Metallica and the band served up a feast. The bond between the band and its metal audience was strong, proving that Metallica had now reached icon status in the genre.

Kirk goes full-on metal during Dynamo Open Air in 1999.

So What
Master Of Puppets
King Nothing
Sad But True
Fuel
Hero Of The Day
Ain't My Bitch
One
Until It Sleeps
For Whom The Bell Tolls
Wherever I May Roam
Nothing Else Matters
Enter Sandman

Stone Cold Crazy
Creeping Death
Battery
Last Caress
Motorbreath

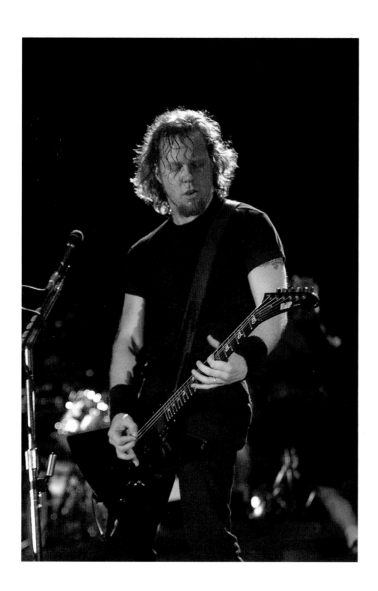

BACK TO BERCY
Paris, France · 7 July 1999

For its big return to France, Metallica again performed at the Palais Omnisports at Bercy, where French crowds had lapped up their performance a few years earlier. The hysterical screams of welcome showed just how eager the fans were to see their idols. The room was plunged into darkness as the sound of Ennio Morricone's song signalled that their patience would soon be rewarded.

Wild. That is perhaps the best way to describe this gig. The Parisian crowd drew its life force from the music and the atmosphere was electric. There was no doubt about it: France was mad for Metallica. The musicians were carried away by the adoration. James, who had been doing much less headbanging at the most recent shows, began bobbing his head at the start of "Master of Puppets", followed by Lars who got up behind his drums, hammering his cymbals like a devil rising from hell.

The first part of the show included 13 tracks. The crowd was insatiable, and Metallica came back on stage three times. This unwavering bond between the band and its French audience was evident when Jason took the floor, drink in hand: 'Come on France, it's good to hear you tonight friends. Thanks for being here tonight with us! Cheers! Salute! Fuck yeah!' Then he threw his beer into the crowd.

Guys
just wanna have fun

Metallica has always played covers. In fact, its very first concerts were ALL covers. The band's genius was that they never admitted to it, mixing covers in with their own songs, leading everyone to believe that they only played originals. A smart move. After notching up seven albums and countless concerts, Metallica released the quirky *Garage Inc.* with a raw, frontal production. The two records feature a collection of songs borrowed from other bands, including Diamond Head, Nick Cave, Discharge, Blue Öyster Cult, Lynyrd Skynyrd and many others. Including a gallery of photos in which the group poses in mechanics' outfits and crisp tuxedos, *Garage Inc.* is a parenthesis. It puts an end to the incessant debate around the release of *Load* and *Reload*. The fans loved it, and *Garage Inc.* sold more than five million copies in the United States alone! In Europe, the record reached number one in the German, Finnish, Norwegian and Swedish charts and got to number nine in France.

WOODSTOCK 1999, GRIFFISS PARK
Rome, New York · 24 July 1999

After a string of concerts in Europe, the band brought its success story home to the United States, with a full-on performance at the revered Woodstock festival held in July to celebrate the 30th anniversary of the iconic event. While the festival was a fiasco due to serious organizational problems, Metallica's performance at the major pop culture event was highly symbolic.

The festival was crowded, with more than 400,000 spectators attending. As he stepped onto the stage, Lars gazed in disbelief at the immense sea of people stretching well beyond the large control tower. A few seconds later, James launched into his now famous: 'So fuckin' what?' and fired the starting gun for a sprint that would become a marathon. The stage was vast. The musicians at the front stood several feet apart, and when Kirk waved his hands at the crowd, the spectators responded with an impressive roar... James taunted the fans, urging them to repeat the song lyrics with him as loudly as possible. The fans packed together in front of the stage struggled to move, giving the mosh pit the appearance of a permanent riot. 'We are Metallica And that's what we do best motherfuckers!' finished James.

Previous page: More than 400,000 visitors gather that day for the third edition of the famous Woodstock festival, and things quickly get out of hand. Left and opposite: Kirk Hammett and Lars Ulrich on the East Stage of the festival, 24 July 1999.

The Woodstock congregation had gathered and James the high priest had spoken, summing up what Metallica had become in the summer of 1999: an unstoppable assault tank that ploughed into the world of rock, pop, metal and thrash, conquering all. In 1999, Metallica was the ultimate global rock supergroup, way ahead of its competitors who were arriving on the scene at the same time in the United States. With eight albums and more than ten tours, the band was a living legend of 1980s and 1990s pop culture, and had nothing more to prove.

As the new century dawned, they could now do whatever they wanted, and that was exactly what they intended to do. Metallica turned to classical music in an effort to blend metal force and symphonic power. They achieved their goal, and then some, with the S&M project.

THE SYMPHONIC
PROJECT

Metallica's stage career took a rather different turn with S&M (Symphony and Metallica). It was more like a slight detour rather than a new direction, because the band gave very few gigs based on this experience. It's easy to understand why.

Though Metallica was used to playing in packed stadiums and going on tours with complex logistics, S&M took things to the next level! The number of musicians, the balance and adjustment times, the importance of acoustics, the absolute concentration; these elements were all vital for the set-up to work, and placed huge limitations on everyone involved. Adding these constraints to venues with restricted capacity – and therefore low profitability – it's easy to understand why the band was unable to take this exciting project on a big road tour.

Setting aside material and financial issues, this symphonic version of Metallica was a big success, both in terms of fan reactions and sales of the double album and the DVD recordings of the symphonic project.

D-3
CONCENTRATION BEFORE THE STORM

Kirk HAMMETT

'It's a challenge. No one expected this from us, and we're taking a risk. That in itself is a statement of some kind.'

The S&M adventure began when the famous conductor Michael Kamen approached the band, with whom he had already worked several times, to suggest a bigger project. Kamen wrote all the arrangements for Metallica's hit "Nothing Else Matters" and his fine reputation as a Hollywood composer meant he was best placed to build a bridge between rock'n'roll and classical music.

Some time later, the Four Horsemen and their staff took up residence at the Berkeley Community Theater in California, three days before the first show, which promised to be spectacular. The musicians were merging two vastly different worlds, in just a few rehearsal sessions. They gave two concerts on 21 and 22 April, and the recording was set for release as a double CD a few months later.

When journalists asked Metallica: 'Did you ever think you would play with a symphony orchestra?' the band members smiled, laughed and thought hard about their

answers. James guffawed openly at the question, while Kirk and Jason admitted to never having considered it. Lars anticipated the criticism that classical music purists might have, and argued that, outside this one project, Metallica did not *play* classical music, but rather *played with* classical music.

Before they began recording, the band was excited, commenting and joking about the difference between the two worlds. 'There is no caviar, there's no champagne, there's no foie gras and we're underpaid!' said Lars, with a glint in his eye, while gorging on a burger. The atmosphere was relaxed but focused. Herbal teas and vocal warm-ups had replaced hard spirits and groupies! Dressed in a crisp T-shirt, James conscientiously worked on his vocals.

The band and conductor prepared for the session behind the scenes on the first day by listening to recordings of Kamen's arrangements. Lars and the others sat on flight cases, deep in concentration, trying to imagine the live rendering of Kamen's work, which he had recorded over the album versions of the titles. The band and the conductor soon got down to some proper rehearsals, surrounded by boxes of equipment. One playing the tracks as if they were rehearsing as normal, the other following his scores, baton in hand, to check the accuracy of his arrangements. It was an astonishing experience, and the contrast between the raw sound of the band and a Karajan-style conductor was striking.

METALLICA &

SAN FRANCISCO SYMPHONY

**PERFORMING METALLICA COMPOSITIONS
ARRANGED & CONDUCTED BY**

MICHAEL KAMEN

APRIL 21 & 22
8PM
BERKELEY COMMUNITY THEATRE

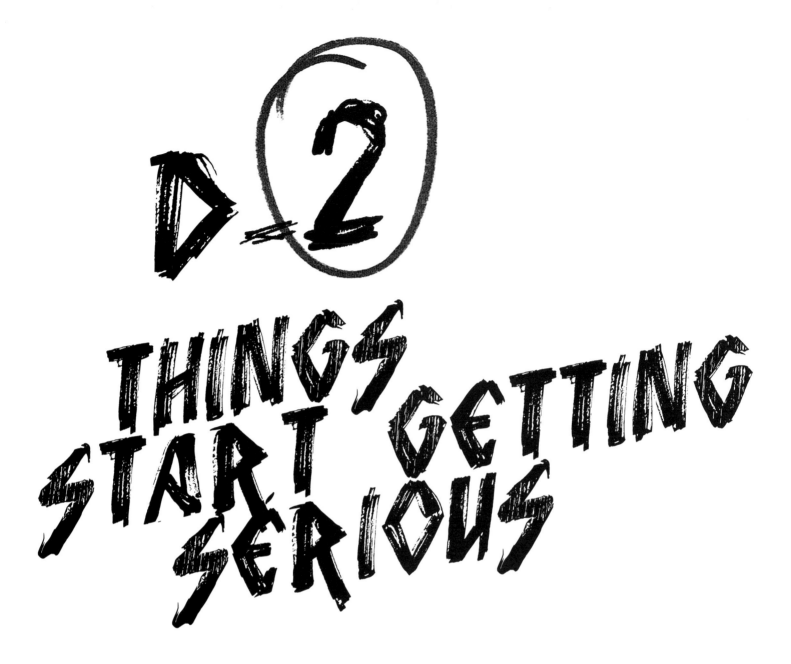

D-2 THINGS START GETTING SERIOUS

The second day was crucial, because Metallica was meeting the musicians in Kamen's orchestra for the first full rehearsals. The streets around the venue were jammed with vans, trucks full of equipment, caravans and trailers. The band was in awe of the venue and its acoustics. 'I think this is just the perfect size, intimate, not too huge,' said a starry-eyed James. Lars seemed more intimidated: 'There's like a hundred-plus of them and four of us!' Kirk was amused to learn where he would be placed among the musicians: 'I'll be in the string section with my own six strings!' Then a technician replied, 'No, woodwind!'
The members of Metallica were like little kids, learning how another style of concert is put together and to comply with the demands of classical music. And when the very first notes of the enchanting arrangement of "Call of Ktulu" resonated, the four friends were blown away by the sound and power of the live orchestra.

Conductor Michael Kamen had already worked in hard rock, including with Metallica on "Nothing Else Matters".

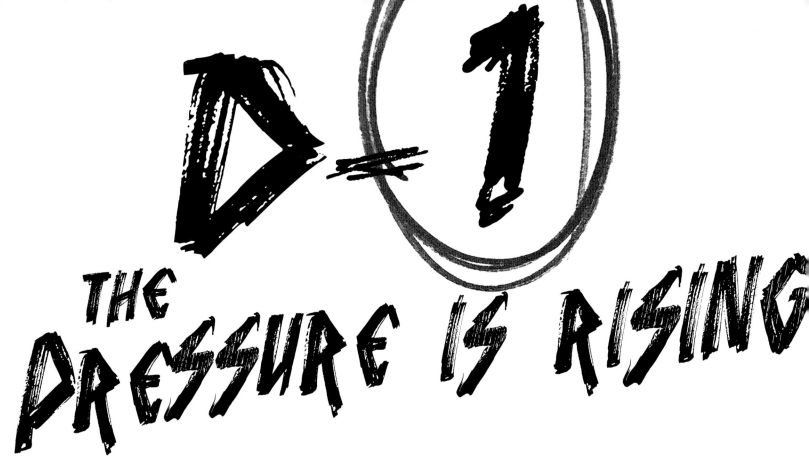

D-1
THE PRESSURE IS RISING

On the third day, some tension began to show, as the members of the band waited in the dressing room in front of their blue metal lockers for their stage costumes to be ironed. It was an opportunity for them to remember high school and the time they spent in marching bands and brass bands.

For the first big dress rehearsal, Metallica was very focused and in awe of the musical talent of the professionals who were playing with them. From behind their music stands, James, Jason and Kirk seemed to be applying themselves like star pupils.

Separated from the others by a Plexiglas wall designed to dull the sound of the drum kit, Lars says 'I think one of the key things for us was that we felt kind of juveniles and I think that we earned their respect.'

When it was time for the dressing-room debrief, Michael Kamen share his feedback with the band, who all listened in respectful silence. It was really something to see four international pop stars, diehard thrashers, take lessons from a wise and scholarly music composer!

Berkeley Community Theater

Located on the campus of Berkeley High School in California, this theatre was built in the late 1940s and opened on 5 June 1950. It is mostly used for school teaching and performances and has just 3,491 seats, which is very few, considering Metallica's capacity to fill stadiums several nights in a row. Unusually, the San Francisco Symphony was not installed in its usual pit for this S&M project, but seated on stage just behind the band. While the venue's main vocation is to educate and put on theatre and classical music productions, Metallica wasn't the first rock band to play here. In 1970, Jimi Hendrix gave two concerts at the venue and the stage has also played host to Led Zeppelin, Bob Dylan, Tangerine Dream, The Grateful Dead, Frank Zappa, Alice Cooper, Elton John and the Eagles, to name only the most famous.

THE BIG DAY

BERKELEY COMMUNITY THEATER
Berkeley, California · 21 April 1999

The timeline for the day was posted on the band's dressing-room door:

- Doors open: 6.30 p.m.
- Metallica: 8 p.m.–9.12 p.m.
- Intermission: 9.12 p.m.–9.27 p.m.
- Metallica: 9.27 p.m.–10.30 p.m.

The schedule was incredibly precise, down to the exact minute, and S&M was probably the only Metallica concert to have an interval!

The usual fans were there, waiting patiently outside the venue. They had had their tickets for a long time, and it was a sellout show. They were all Metallica devotees, but many of them were wondering what the band had in store for them this time. Some wore T-shirts and banners with the effigy of their favourite band, others ditched their black jeans and T-shirt and went dressier, as if they had seats at the opera!

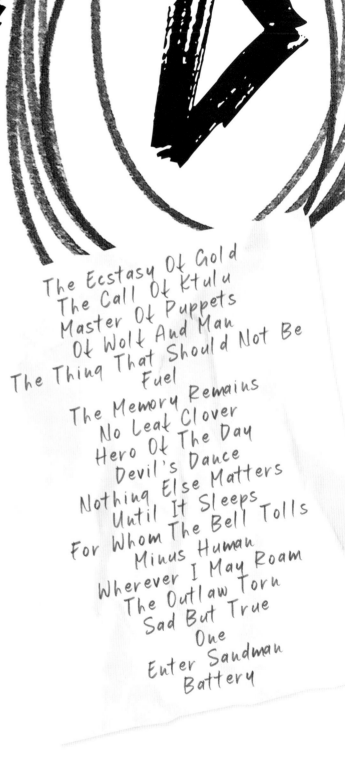

The Ecstasy Of Gold
The Call Of Ktulu
Master Of Puppets
Of Wolf And Man
The Thing That Should Not Be
Fuel
The Memory Remains
No Leaf Clover
Hero Of The Day
Devil's Dance
Nothing Else Matters
Until It Sleeps
For Whom The Bell Tolls
Minus Human
Wherever I May Roam
The Outlaw Torn
Sad But True
One
Enter Sandman
Battery

When the artists took their places on stage, the contrast couldn't have been greater between James astride his Harley Davidson and the calm and confident arrival of the orchestra musicians in their crisp white shirts, blazers and trousers! The hunt for autographs outside the venue was on, and Lars – dressed in a simple mauve robe – enjoyed indulging the fans. Unlike the band's other concerts, the S&M venue had seating, like an opera. But that didn't stop the fans from squealing with delight when they saw the venue and the stage. And when the musicians arrived on stage, the crowd was on its feet to applaud the 100 members of the symphony orchestra, stoic at their stands, clarinets and violins in hand.

James emerged first, while the orchestra played the legendary introductory music by Ennio Morricone. Lars waited in the wings, then sat at his drum kit as the first bars of the introduction to "Call of Ktulu" rang out. Visibly tense with a clenched jaw, Jason waited at the side, bass in hand, then climbed to the stage calmly, reverently. The band members caught each other's eye as the sumptuous arrangement unfolded, then exploded in a shower of distorted guitars and clashing cymbals. The audience was enthralled, and the yelling drowned out the beginning of this legendary track. Their early restraint forgotten, the fans were now almost all on their feet. There was no doubt about it, this was a genuine Metallica gig!

The lucky spectators were treated to almost two and a half hours of thrills. Even well-known tracks took on a new and unknown character, especially the fiercest ones. "Call of Ktulu" became a mythological sea serpent that grew horns through lyrical soaring strings. This was more than a Metallica show. It was a gig that honoured the band's achievements and was performed by classical players who enhanced the music rather than drawing attention to themselves. On this night, the music itself – not the band – was the star of the show. The lead-in to "Master of Puppets" was magnified by the classical arrangement, and this legendary thrash hit conjured up scenes of a chariot race in a Hollywood epic. The cinematic

dimension of the band's songs was revealed during a set that combined titles from the latest albums ("Fuel", "The Outlaw Torn"), iconic hits ("Sad But True", "Battery", "Enter Sandman") and unreleased tracks like "No Leaf Clover" which was played live for the very first time that evening. After an hour and a quarter of music that came to a head with "Bleeding", Metallica left the stage for a 15-minute interval. The house lights came up, illuminating the orchestra's music stands and empty seats. Even though the crowd had been told about the interval, it was clearly a novelty for the band's fans, because they went on shouting and screaming throughout.

About 15 minutes later, everyone was back on stage and Michael Kamen, baton in hand, gave the start for an anthological "Nothing Else Matters". The famous arpeggio played by Kirk Hammett was magnificently highlighted with layers of silky string playing. Sitting on a stool, acoustic guitar in hand, James Hetfield sang better than he ever had, and managed to convey the full emotion of the ballad in a completely new way. The band followed up with "Until It Sleeps", "For Whom the Bell Tolls" and seven other tracks, including the huge hits "One" and "Enter Sandman". The set wrapped with a thunderous version of "Battery", and James finished by shouting 'Thank you

Michael Kamen, the Hollywood Wizard

Having trained at the prestigious Juilliard School in New York, Michael Kamen played the oboe before turning his hand to conducting, and devoting his entire career to the art. From the very beginning, he showed a surprising talent for bringing rock and classical music together, founding the New York group Rock & Roll Ensemble. He released a total of five records as part of the project. He then composed a series of soundtracks for Hollywood blockbusters, including *Brazil*, *Highlander*, *Lethal Weapon*, *Die Hard*, *Licence to Kill*, *Robin Hood*, *Prince of Thieves* and *X-Men*. His first collaboration with Metallica dates to the *Black Album*, on which he arranged the ballad "Nothing Else Matters". After S&M, he performed with other rock groups and artists including Aerosmith, Pink Floyd, Sting, David Bowie, Kate Bush, Bryan Adams, Queen, Eurythmics, Queensrÿche and Lenny Kravitz.

friends yeah!' to a shower of screams and applause. Fists raised, the fans also celebrated the orchestra. All the musicians stood up from behind their music stands to acknowledge the audience. Visibly moved, Hetfield got the fans to show their appreciation for these exceptional musicians who had brought a new dimension to Metallica's work. Michael Kamen joined the band on stage to greet a captivated audience while Lars and Kirk gazed around the room, beaming.

Back in the dressing rooms, the band was high on the thrill of taking this symphonic journey through their music catalogue. With misty eyes and proud grins, Metallica were delighted. As they left the venue, fan feedback was unanimous: 'epic', 'incredible', 'fantastic', there was no shortage of superlatives from the crowd. But it wasn't over. The band and the orchestra gave a second sold-out concert the next day. Their idea was to have two live versions of each track so they could select the best one for the *S&M* record that would be released the following No-

vember. By 23 November, everything was in the can. They celebrated the event with a third symphony show, this time in New York.

Later, Kirk explained that the project went ahead 'because it's a new challenge for us. It breaks the continuity of recording, performing, recording. It's new. The option to record with a symphonic orchestra, it's a great thing. It is in fact not the first time it's been done, the connection between rock and a symphony orchestra, but when Deep Purple did it, it was different. Because we take old and known songs, and put them up with the orchestra. They did new things, that weren't necessarily received well.'

On the subject of "routine", which all great rock bands know, Lars went even further: 'You know, the thing about the symphony stuff... part of what makes it really cool is the fact that it's not something that ends up being sort of overkill. I don't want to go on tour with this record for 100 dates. It's a great thing to be able to come back to and do once in a while in special situations, you know, "It's 2002

S&M2:
20 years later

The band was now celebrating 20 years since S&M, a magical moment in their career. In 2019 they decided to go through it all again with a second symphonic production.

Once again, the band collaborated with the San Francisco Philharmonic Symphony, whose players brought a new sound to its music. As Michael Kamen had passed away in 2003, the project was now managed by Edwin Outwater and Michael Tilson Thomas. The production was recorded live on 6 and 8 September 2019 at the Chase Theater in San Francisco. The film based on this project was released on 9 October and the album on 28 August of the following year. Tracks included versions of "Call of Ktulu" and "Master of Puppets" as well as new arrangements ("The Day That Never Comes", "Confusion", "All Within My Hands").

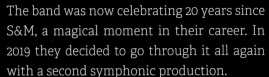

and we're down in Australia for two weeks, let's go play one with the Sydney Symphony Orchestra," that type of thing. But to go out and sort of tour it? No. I think that would take away from the speciality vibe of the whole thing. [...] It's a lot more intense. Nobody probably wants to hear this, but when you're playing your eighth show in Germany in ten days, sometimes the mind can wander a little. The two shows in Berkeley with the San Francisco Orchestra... that was about as focused as I've ever been onstage, in terms of wanting to hold down our part of it and not screw up and not let the team down. I guess it's one thing, letting a team of four down. Another is letting a team of 108 down...'

'That's what I remember about the two shows: a complete inner focus and really just dealing with my aspect of it and not wondering about the lights or the pretty girl in row three, and really just holding down my end of it more so than ever. That's the ugly truth.'

As the 20th century drew to a close, Metallica prepared to take a break as Lars announced to the press: 'January 9 in an unnamed city in the Midwest of the US will be the last Metallica commitment for a long time. [...] I think it's been six years since we were staring at a schedule that was blank. We put out four records in four years now, and we always have something in front of us, and this is the first time that we don't have anything in front of us.' In 2000, the band took a proper break. But this was also the year of the "Napster affair" when Metallica went head-to-head with the illegal download file browser. To make matters worse, at the start of the following year, on 17 January, Jason Newsted announced that he was leaving the band, then in July, James checked into a rehab centre to treat his chronic alcohol addiction. It was the beginning of a period of turmoil for the group, which reached its peak when the band went into "therapy" with performance-enhancement coach Phil Towle while Metallica were recording the new album. The documentary which was initially supposed to be just a behind-the-scenes view of how the record got made, gradually turned into a sad farce during which the members of Metallica tore themselves apart in writing sessions and revealed their arguments in cringeworthy footage. The chaos continued for two years and only came to an end with the release of *St. Anger*, produced by Bob Rock, on 5 June 2003.

ANGER
AND A RESURRECTION

The final part of this incredible saga sees the band reach a kind of stage maturity worthy of the greatest 21st-century pop stars. Though the three albums released between 2003 and 2016 continued to divide fans, Metallica was still an unstoppable live-performing machine, and a string of legendary shows punctuated this chapter in their story. It was the era of iconic concerts with the Rolling Stones, the tour that reunites the Big Four of Trash, the very first concerts in China, and the atypical performances that only big guns could handle, like the one in Antarctica.

These key gigs made Metallica a phenomenon of pop culture.

AFTER THE STORM

After three years of turmoil, Metallica saw the release of *St. Anger* as a renaissance. In 2003, the band returned to the stage with a new bassist: Robert Trujillo. With festivals in Europe, club dates in France, the United States, South America and then Australia, it seemed like Metallica was back for good! The band definitely made its comeback when the United States and world tour, Madly in Anger with the World, was launched in February to promote the *St. Anger* album.

Blackened
Fuel
Harvester of Sorrow
Welcome Home (Sanitarium)
For Whom the Bell Tolls
Frantic
King Nothing
Dirty Window
Sad But True
Creeping Death
Battery
St. Anger
Guitar solo
Nothing Else Matters
Master of Puppets
One
Enter Sandman
Last Caress
Hit the Lights

BACK FROM HELL
AT AMERICA WEST ARENA
Phoenix, Arizona · 2 March 2004

This new tour with its very explicit name was one of Metallica's legendary marathons, taking in countless venues around the United States in early 2004. It kicked off at Cow Palace in San Francisco on 27 February, then moved to the America West Arena in Phoenix, Arizona on 2 March.

Metallica brought out a brand-new stage for this tour. In a bid to reconnect with the raw thrash and rock style of the new album, the band designed a platform that allowed fans to surround them completely. The band members all stood around Lars and his drum kit and low-level lighting picked out each player individually, adding to the pared-down effect.

After the performance by Godsmack, who opened for Metallica on this tour, the America West Arena was plunged into darkness. The now trademark music by Ennio Mor-

ricone rang out and the fans could sense that the magic was about to happen. But tonight, instead of the traditional opener "Master of Puppets", the intro to "Blackened" burst from the speakers. This was a first for the band, even though it had always played tracks from …*And Justice for All*. It was an innovative move to open the set with this ice-cold slice of pure relentless thrash. It was a challenge for a band that had weathered so many storms, with many of its fans fearing that the band's return would be a let-down.

In the harsh white spotlight beams the band launched headlong into their new tour, backed up by the crowd who sang with James, fists pumping the air with each 'Blackened'! At the iconic mid-track break, Lars pummelled his bass drum and fans around the central stage went into a trance, headbanging wildly to the rhythm of

this legendary riff. Longtime Metallica devotees were relieved and satisfied.

The band prowled around Lars, like lions in a cage, stirring up the audience. Robert Trujillo had already notched up several concerts over the last few months with his new band and he gave his all to this performance, providing a solid foundation with finger playing that kept the band perfectly in time. By hiring him, Metallica earned a top-quality bass player; his imposing stature was a great match for the trio. The new bassist even joined in on backing vocals, just like Jason Newsted. Unsurprisingly, the gig was perfectly executed, and even though signs of the passing years may have started to show on their faces, their stage presence was as fresh as ever.

As the new tour name suggests, Metallica was indeed "angry", but this anger was healthy. The introduction to the next track set that in stone. It was another new entry, with the addition of pyrotechnic effects all around the stage when Lars started striking his drums.

Don't worry, Metallica fans, your favourite musicians still had plenty of fire in their bellies. This live performance masterclass lasted almost two hours and set the tone for a triumphant tour which saw the band playing more than 80 shows around North America. They then flew to Europe for the rest of this Madly in Anger with the World Tour.

James and Lars during the Madly in Anger with the World Tour, here at the Cow Palace in San Francisco 8 March, 2004

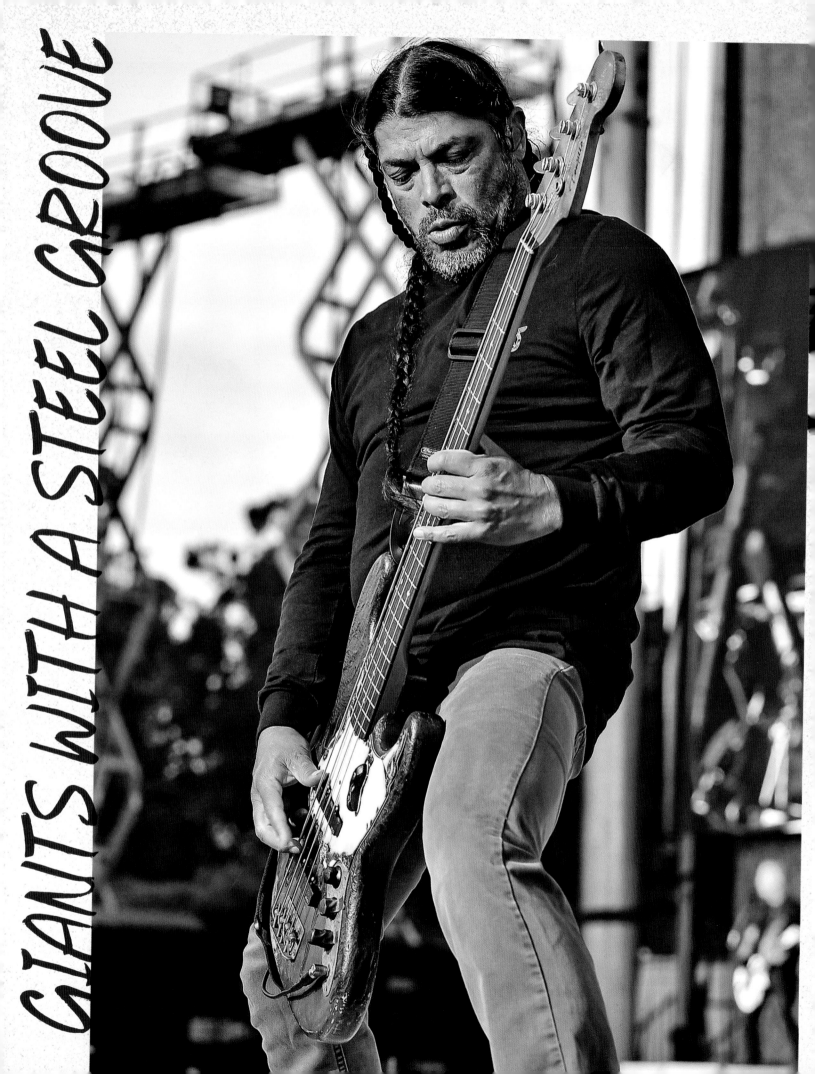

GIANTS WITH A STEEL GROOVE

ROBERT TRUJILLO

'It's like Rob has guitar picks for fingers.' That is how Lars Ulrich described Robert Trujillo's playing after the bassist auditioned for the band in 2003.

Born in Santa Monica, California on 23 October 1964 to a mother of Mexican origin, the future bassist quickly became fascinated by the talent of his flamenco-playing guitarist father. Robert tried to imitate him, but eventually felt most comfortable on the bass.

In 1989, he became a member of Suicidal Tendencies and quickly got a reputation for a playing style packed with groove and power. These two qualities were essential to the style of the bands he joined or founded, such as Infectious Grooves. Just listen to the introduction to "Violent and Funky". Robert is a genuine virtuoso.

In 2003, almost two years after Jason had left the Four Horsemen, Robert auditioned for Metallica and it was love at first sight. 'We all felt this incredible magic between the four of us. It was just something that we could not describe, we all just knew it.' He was officially inducted as Metallica's bassist on 24 February 2003, a position he holds to this day. He stands tall on stage, then crawls around almost at ground level like a snake weaving between two venomous groove lines.

[THEY] LOVE PARIS
AT PARC DES PRINCES
Paris, France · 23 June 2004

The Metallica machine landed in Europe and toured from 14 to 31 May, taking in Denmark, Finland, Sweden and Poland. It then called at several festivals (including Castle Donington in the United Kingdom and Rock in Rio in Portugal) before heading to Eastern Europe (Germany, Switzerland, Austria, Serbia, etc.).

On 23 June, the band made its big comeback in France, not counting the three dates it had played in Parisian clubs the previous year. This June, the world's biggest metal band had a date with one of its most devoted crowds at the bustling Parc des Princes stadium in Paris, and for French fans of metal, it was a very special night! Two other heavyweight bands were scheduled: Lostprophets and most importantly Slipknot, who at the time were on their way up.

The musicians got ready to perform as dusk fell. The stage was very different from the one they had been using on the Madly in Anger with the World Tour in the United States. They performed on a huge set at one end of the stadium, and the set-up bore a striking resemblance to the band's beginnings in the mid-1980s. The staging was traditional and understated, with two giant screens projecting the action to the fans at the very back. The Parc was packed that night, the playing field crammed, and the stands almost completely full.

Previous page: Lars, Robert, Kirk and James rehearse backstage during a tour around the United States, 19 July 2003.
Opposite: The ESP KH-2 M-II known as Boris Karloff Mummy graphic, Kirk's favourite guitar.

Blackened
Fuel
Sad But True
Fade to Black
Frantic
Holier Than Thou
I Disappear
Wherever I May Roam
St. Anger
Creeping Death
Battery
No Leaf Clover
Guitar Solo
Nothing Else Matters
Master of Puppets
One
Enter Sandman
Dyers Eve
Seek and Destroy

As usual, the French fans threw themselves into the gig, singing along right from the first bars of the intro, even before the band appeared on stage! When "Blackened" began, the fans responded in a roar, recognizing it immediately, and a forest of arms sprouted from the stadium. In this conventional stadium set-up and playing an old-school track, Metallica reassured its fans that they were proud of their roots and their past, no matter what their critics said. This "vintage" feel was underscored by the walls of amps lining the back of the stage, at a time when digital guitar processing reigned supreme.

After just one track, the French audience was putty in their hands, roaring with delight. 'Paris! Metallica is with

you! Are you with us? Give me an M! Give me an E! Give me a T!' James shouted to the crowd, launching "Load" with its immense flames. 'It's so good to see you again! Metallica feels so good that Paris wants more of Metallica! Thank you very very much, Metallica is very grateful to be here after 22 years and seeing all these friends from France. [...] Thank you!'

The band's declaration of love to its French fans set the tone for the gig that evening, and James sealed an unbreakable bond that has lasted for many years. When

Lars launched into "Sad But True", its humongous riff now supported by Trujillo's pure groove bassline, the Parc des Princes was an ocean of headbangers.

The reunion between Metallica and the French crowd lasted for over two hours and 15 minutes. The Four Horsemen had worked their magic once again. Despite lacklustre albums, scandals and criticism, despite the advancing age of the band – and their fans – the performance was a roaring success. France and Metallica were clearly still firm friends.

Lars Ulrich misses the 2004 Download Festival, so Slipknot's bass player Joey Jordison fills in on the drums, saving Metallica's Donington Park show.

LAST BUT NOT LEAST: HP PAVILION
San Jose, California · 28 November 2004

After Paris, the band continued its journey through Europe before hitting the road again in the United States for the last major leg of this Madly in Anger with the World Tour. The band began its journey on 16 August in Saint Paul, Minnesota and wrapped up on 28 November in San Jose, California, after a total of 50 concerts; once again an average of one gig every two days! It was an impressive feat for a group of musicians who had spent most of their time living the high life on tour buses and in hotel rooms.

The logistics for this North American leg of the tour to promote *St. Anger* were mind-blowing. 'We have three different stages, with six different crews: one Universal crew that goes to all of the shows, primarily travelling on a chartered jet (the band's personal techs, etc.); two identical "Black" and "Blue" crews that leapfrog their way around the country, looking over the stage set-up at alternating shows; and finally, three "steel" crews who actually arrive days in advance of each gig to build the stages themselves. Throw in 36 tour buses and 50+ 18-wheelers, and you've got yourself a multi-million dollar summer entertainment package!'

Mind-blowing. This gigantic circus arrived in San Jose, California on 28 November 2004 for the last day of the American tour. The atmosphere in the dressing rooms was relaxed but studious. The band warmed up together before each live performance and even had a small rehearsal room set aside.

That evening, Metallica rehearsed "Blackened", the track that had opened their set list for several months. It came as no surprise to anyone that this show was a triumph, and the band made no bones about how much they were enjoying themselves, running from one track to another with delighted precision, as evidenced in "Disposable Heroes", which was played seventh. The cult hit from *Master of Puppets* proved – if it were necessary – that despite their status as international rock stars, James and his band were still capable of delivering assaults of pure thrash after more than 19 months on the road and 180 concerts. After this tour de force, the band said farewell to the stage and would not be back again until almost a year later, for a very special event.

Previous page: Robert Trujillo on the Sport Authority Field stage at Mile High in Denver, Colorado, 7 June 2017. Opposite: Kirk and James backstage at the Amsterdam Arena, 21 June 2004.

CLASH OF THE TITANS: SBC PARK
San Francisco, California
13 and 14 November 2005

These two shows, which sealed the band's status as global icons, saw Metallica opening two nights in a row for the unparalleled legends of rock: the Rolling Stones. Metallica was only given a 30-minute slot for these two very special shows, just like old times! The only difference being that this time the band hammered out all their most mainstream midtempo classics. "No Leaf Clover", "Sad But True", "Fade to Black", "One", "Nothing Else Matters", "Enter Sandman" and so on. The only concession to their thrash period was "Master of Puppets", played second. The track made a strong impression on an audience that was more accustomed to conventional rock than 100 per cent metal-armoured onslaughts.

Lars Ulrich described these two shows in 2019: 'Fourteen years ago today, on 13 November 2005, we got back up on stage after almost a year away. We opened for an up-and-coming British rock band called the Rolling Stones at two concerts in San Francisco. The *St. Anger* tour had ended a year before that, and after some much needed time off, we got the call just as we were getting ready to work on the band's next creative phase. Until that point, we had played with a lot of bands whose posters I'd had on my walls, including Deep Purple, AC/DC, Iron Maiden and so on, and I was delighted to get the opportunity to rock with Stones at home in San Francisco. Playing two shows, going on stage early, not promoting anything, doing a shorter set, and then heading back to my bed at home, it was a really great vibe and a cool way to kick off the creation of the next album. It was an inspiring and memorable experience!'

These were the only two concerts Metallica played in 2005.

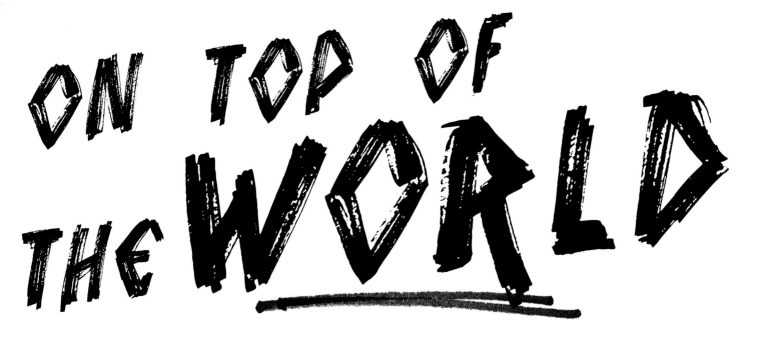

ON TOP OF THE WORLD

A lot had changed for Metallica. There were no more endless world tours as soon as a new album was released. The band allowed itself to take yearlong breaks, as it did in 2005. In 2006, the musicians hit the road again for a European tour, taking in several festivals and three dates in Japan. In 2007, they only toured in the summer months, and mainly in Europe. Over the course of two years, the band only performed 31 concerts. The pace picked up again in 2008 with the release of a ninth album on 12 September: *Death Magnetic*.

That Was Just Your Life
The End of the Line
Creeping Death
Harvester of Sorrow
One
Broken, Beat & Scarred
Cyanide
Sad But True
The Unforgiven
All Nightmare Long
The Day That Never Comes
Master of Puppets
Damage, Inc.
Nothing Else Matters
Enter Sandman
Last Caress
Green Hell
Seek and Destroy

A CLOSE ENCOUNTER OF THE THIRD KIND
AT THE GREAT WESTERN FORUM
Los Angeles, California
17 December 2008

The World Magnetic Tour gave the Four Horsemen a chance to get back in the touring saddle after three years at a gentle trot. Metallica had North America on its radar, with 36 gigs planned through to the following February. After travelling through Arizona, New Mexico, Missouri, Iowa, Oregon, Utah, Colorado, Nebraska, Illinois, Ohio, Oklahoma, Texas, Arkansas, Louisiana and Washington, the band flew to Canada on 2 December to perform four concerts then returned to California for a handful of one-off shows.

On 17 December, the musicians were on top form when they took to the stage at the Great Western Forum. The atmosphere was almost mystical. The concert began in a bluish glow, a guitar arpeggio introducing the opening track on the most recent album: "That Was Just Your Life". Metallica were clearly not going to settle for all-time clas-

sics on this tour! They were determined to get their fans on board with this new record and have them understand that they were back for good. Blinding flashes and laser beams knifed through the air as the song's fierce thrash riff got going.

The 2000s had had an impact on the staging style. Precise lightshows manicured to every beat of the music created a true spectacle for the fans. This tour was a sign that Metallica had its finger on the pulse.

As the devilish first thrash track unfolded, a UFO bathed in futuristic light took off, plunging the musicians near-darkness, except for James who was singing. As the concert opened, the star of the show was clearly the music itself rather than the players. Blinding lights eventually went up in the arena as James shouted 'Los Angeles! It's your life! It's your life!'

The fans finally got to see more of the stage during "The End of The Line" (the second track on *Death Magnetic*). Here, Lars was a central magnet for the other three musicians, who gravitated around him like neutrons around an atom, each lit by a white followspot on a riotous background of bright colours. As the band was clearly focusing on pure thrash'n'roll, the second track sparked an avalanche of raised fists and furious headbanging among the most hardcore fans who were packed into the front rows, crammed against the crash barriers. Kirk delivered an unbridled solo drowned in wah-wah pedals, recalling the heyday of 80s metal!

The crowd went wild when James reassured his audience: 'Metallica is alive and well and here to kick some ass!!!', a clear message backed up in the third track, "Creeping Death", one of the highlights of the gig, which proved to even their most cynical fans that Metallica could still deliver its most aggressive bombs with unwavering ferocity. After this series in California, the band picked up the tour again in January, flying to Europe in February where they played a concert in Nottingham, England on the 25th of the month.

Bringing Robert Trujillo on board, Metallica gains a top-quality bass player, his imposing stature a great match for the quartet.

Death Magnetic: back to basics?

There was no room for error after *St. Anger*. Metallica had to come up with the goods. They knew they couldn't go more mainstream than *Load/Reload*, nor repeat the Herculean feat achieved by the *Black Album* hit machine, so Metallica made a horizontal move, recording a very raw record which marks a clear return to the band's roots: fast tempos, thrash overlaps and an aggressive, almost sloppy production result, which places the guitars front and centre in the mix. The album produced with Rick Rubin was released on 12 September 2008 and has the distinction of being the first on which new member Robert Trujillo records the bass lines. Quickly (as is often the case with Metallica), controversy arose about the sound of the record, which some describe as saturated. This was due to overcompression during the mixing process, which makes the album overpowering from start to finish. Some might say it lacks depth and dynamics. Even so, *Death Magnetic* does contain a few bombshells that wreak havoc during concerts, like the album's opening track, "That Was Just Your Life".

GLADIATORS IN NÎMES ARENA
Nîmes, France · 7 July 2009

This was an unforgettable show for the lucky French fans who got to attend. The combination of the legendary band and an iconic Roman arena in the ancient city of Nîmes made the event very special. The performance was recorded and released as a DVD entitled "Français pour une nuit".

As dusk fell and the introduction to the concert began, the almost magical atmosphere of the place created a uniquely solemn mood. With one voice, like a Roman legion, the colossal crowd chanted every note of Ennio Morricone's music, then burst into a deafening roar when Lars, Kirk, James and Robert finally arrived on stage. Hair slicked back and gleaming like a gladiator, James let the audience finish each chorus of the first track, "Blackened", and celebrated with a raised fist when Lars marked the tempo of the legendary break.

It was war in the mosh pit. Unlike the United States tour, when the band kicked off with two tracks from *Death Magnetic*, this time it looked like Metallica wanted to please an audience with whom they had maintained a special relationship since the beginning. They cemented this by following on with "Creeping Death", another classic. The fans sang all the guitar riffs and obviously knew every song from the band's early days by heart. The roars never subsided, even between tracks. "Fade to Black", "Sad But True", "One", "Master of Puppets", "Nothing Else Matters", "Enter Sandman" and so on. All the classics made up a practically perfect set list before the band wrapped up with the devastating diptych "Motorbreath"/"Seek & Destroy". Unforgettable.

The tour went on through the summer of 2009 with dates in Spain, Portugal, Switzerland, Sweden, Denmark, Finland, Norway and England, before returning to the United States in September.

Like gladiators, James and Kirk take to the stage with the ancient arena of Nîmes in the background.

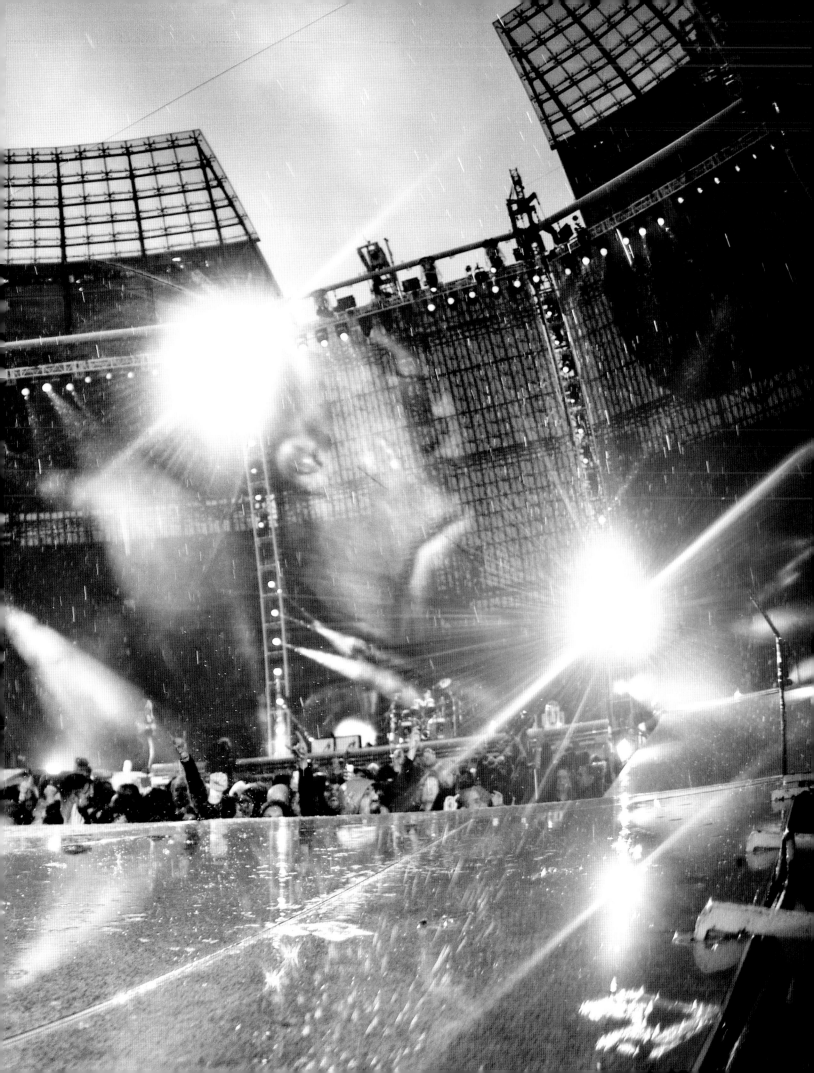

ROCK AND ROLL HALL OF FAME
MADISON SQUARE GARDEN

New York, New York · 30 October 2009

When the band was invited alongside other rock super-stars to celebrate the 25th anniversary of the Rock and Roll Hall of Fame, Metallica could rest assured they'd reached legendary status. It was an all-American show with iconic guests and a set list of timeless hits. Lou Reed, the living legend of 70s rock, shared the microphone with James on two tracks, and Metallica performed two Black Sabbath covers with ex-band member Ozzy looking on. The invitation to attend this gathering of the rock glitterati showed the world that Metallica was well and truly part of the American pop establishment. They rubbed shoulders with U2, The Black Eyed Peas, Patti Smith, Bruce Springsteen, Jeff Beck, Buddy Guy, Billy Gibbons, Sting, Aretha Franklin, Annie Lennox and Lenny Kravitz. But there was no sign of glitz and glam on the forthcoming 2010 tour...

For Whom the Bell Tolls
One
Turn the Page
Sweet Jane (+ Lou Reed)
WhiteLight/White Heat
(+ Lou Reed)
Iron Man (+ Ozzy Osbourne)
Paranoid (+ Ozzy Osbourne)
You Really Got Me (+ Ray Davies)
All Day and All of the
Night (+ Ray Davies)
Stone Cold Crazy
Enter Sandman

Previous page: Light years from the atmosphere in the ancient Nîmes amphitheatre, Metallica performs at the Olympic stadium in Berlin (Germany) on 6 July 2019.
Above: Twenty-three years later, Ozzy Osbourne and Metallica meet again on stage at Madison Square Garden.
Opposite: That same day, Lou Reed shares the microphone with James for two songs.

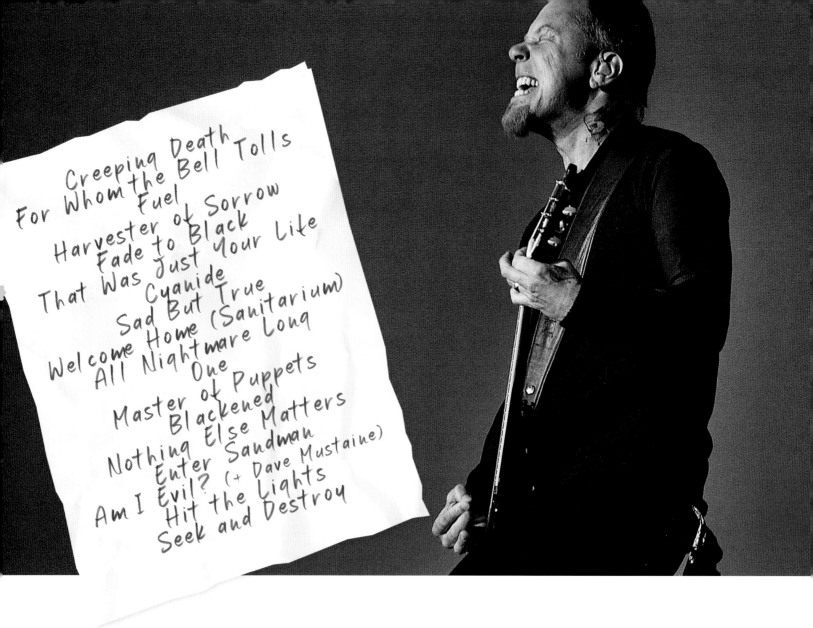

OLD FRIENDS AT LEVSKI STADIUM
Sofia, Bulgaria · 22 June 2010

June 2010 brought an event eagerly awaited by all metal fans. It was the very first tour with the "Big Four of Thrash": Slayer, Anthrax, Megadeth and Metallica. This mammoth set-up was preparing to travel across Europe and around the world for a reunion of the best US bands to celebrate the early thrash scene. After Warsaw on the 16th, the Sonisphere festival in Switzerland on the 18th and Prague on the 19th, the Big Four arrived to perform at the stadium in Sofia, Bulgaria.

For this exceptional tour, Metallica chose a set list mainly composed of the biggest hits from its most legendary albums. And even though technically the band included this series of shows in its World Magnetic promotional tour, the musicians were going all out with timeless classics. As such, the set burst open with a devastatingly energetic "Creeping Death".

No surprises: the Sofia stadium was packed and the stage gigantic. Under the Bulgarian capital's stormy sky, huge screens at the back of the stage and either side broadcast images to those at the back who couldn't see. The band had ditched the fancy light shows they used for World Magnetic in the United States, and the stage was bathed in light, each musician in their own followspot.

James lifted his microphone stand during the last chorus: 'Sofia! It's up to you!' He then let the audience chant back the words. 'Is the Metallica family here? Is the Metallica family here?' said James at the end of this incredible introduction, before the band launched into a masterful performance of "For Whom the Bell Tolls" with (and this was new) the famous introductory melodic motif impeccably played on bass by an inventive Robert Trujillo. In the middle of the set came an anthology of five hits: "One", "Master of Puppets", "Blackened", "Nothing Else Matters", "Enter Sandman".

The band was on top form for this series of exceptional shows, and invited Dave Mustaine and the musicians from the other bands that evening to share the stage during "Am I Evil?". The guitarists and bassists lined the front of the stage, headbanging to the rhythm of the classic thrash hit.

The four bands carried on to Athens and Bucharest, before ending the Big Four 2010 tour in Istanbul. Metallica then had the Pacific in its sights, heading off on the long trip to Australia, New Zealand and Japan through to November, when they returned to the United States to break for a few months.

THE FILLMORE: HAPPY 30!
San Francisco, California
10 December 2011

The gig to celebrate the band's 30th anniversary was one of a kind. Metallica had pulled out all the stops, inviting musician friends, former members and various guests to put together an unforgettable show. The atmosphere was relaxed right from the start. Members of the current line-up shared jokes into the microphone and thanked the audience.

James, Lars and Kirk had plenty of surprises in store. The band played the first seven tracks as it would in a regular gig. But when the time came for "Dirty Window" and "Frantic", the star producer Bob Rock took the bass, as he did for a time after Jason left the band. Then came three covers of legendary Black Sabbath hits, played with Ozzy himself and Geezer Butler, the band's bassist. Next up was Jason Newsted, who came to play "King Nothing" and "Whiplash".

But the highlight of the evening was the very last portion of the set, when Dave Mustaine joined his ex-bandmates for "Phantom Lord", "Jump in the Fire", "Metal Militia", "Hit the Lights" and "Seek & Destroy." The final two tracks were a real family reunion with all the former members

of the band joining Metallica on stage (Dave Mustaine, Lloyd Grant and Ron McGovney on "Hit the Lights" and Dave Mustaine, Jason Newsted, Lloyd Grant and Ron McGovney on "Seek & Destroy"). Unforgettable!

Above: Metallica's two bassists – Jason Newsted and Robert Trujillo – share the microphone for one song.
Next page: Ron McGovney and Dave Mustaine reunite with their former partners, seen here with Lloyd Grant.

The handwritten setlist:

Orion
Through the Never
Ride the Lightning
The God That Failed
Welcome Home (Sanitarium)
Rebel of Babylon
Blackened
Dirty Window
Frantic
Sabbra Cadabra
Iron Man
Paranoid
King Nothing
Whiplash
Motorbreath
Phantom Lord
Jump in the Fire
Metal Militia
Hit the Lights
Seek and Destroy

ORION MUSIC + MORE
Atlantic City, New Jersey
23 and 24 April 2012

Metallica went on touring throughout 2011, then in 2012 embarked on one of its trademark mammoth projects. The band wanted to organize their own festival in the United States. The major event needed to include no fewer than four stages, each bearing the name of one of its songs ("Orion", "Fuel", "Damage Inc.", "Frantic"). The line-up included 37 bands, with artists such as Arctic Monkeys, Ghost, Avenged Sevenfold, Suicidal Tendencies, Sepultura, A Place to Bury Strangers, Hot Snakes and so on.

The icing on the cake was that Metallica was set to play two nights in a row as headliners! If you want something done, do it yourself.
On Saturday 24 April, the band performed the entire *Ride the Lightning* album for the first time and the next day the Four Horsemen played through the legendary *Black Album*. The jubilee event was sold out and attracted 23,571 spectators.

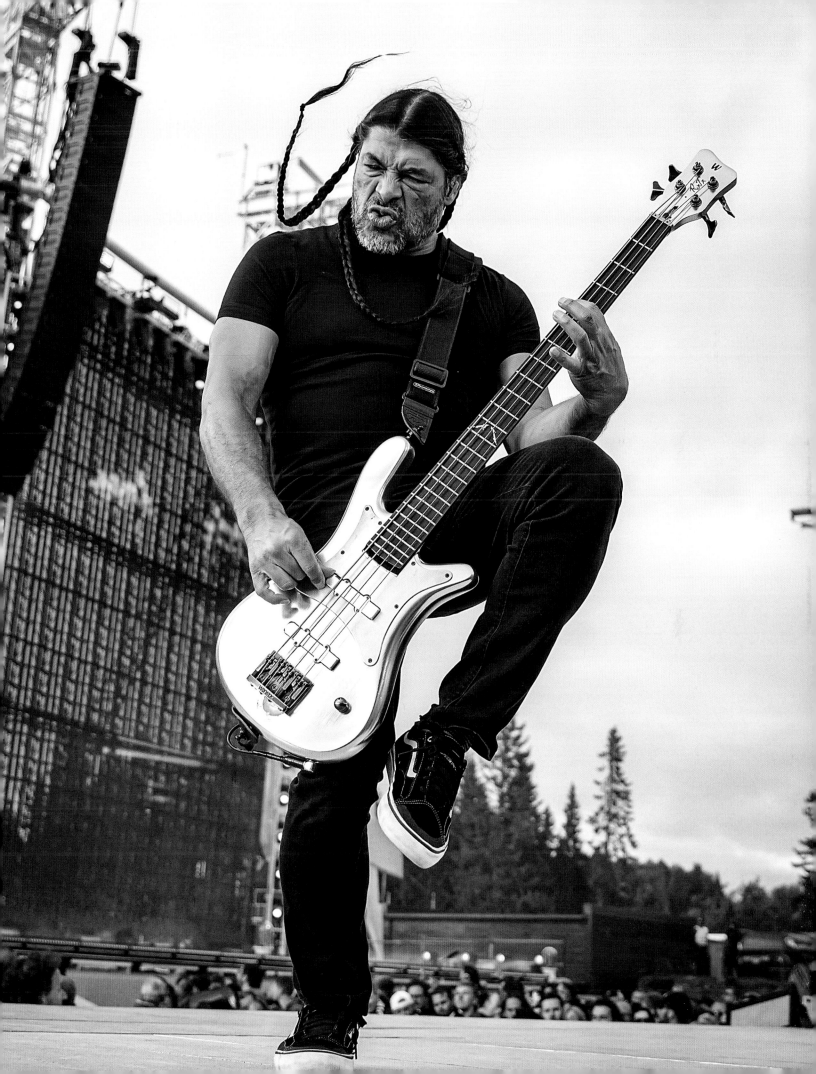

MERCEDES-BENZ ARENA
Shanghai, China · 13 August 2013

At the start of 2013, Metallica embarked on a world tour, this time mainly in the Southern Hemisphere and Asia. In February, the band went to Australia for five concerts, then made a stopover in Abu Dhabi on 19 April and performed just a single show there before flying to South Africa for three more gigs.

At the beginning of the summer, after a detour to the United States and Denmark, the band finally launched its attack on Asia, starting with Japan. On 13 August the boys were invited to play at the Mercedes-Benz Arena in Shanghai, China. A first for the Four Horsemen. Despite playing internationally for many years, even making regular visits to Asia, the band had never been able to book a single show in the country. The 18,000 tickets sold out in a flash, proving that the band had built up an impressive Chinese fanbase without doing any live shows in the country.

Before the gig, blue chairs were lined up in neat rows across the pit, and when the evening began, the band happily agreed to sign autographs backstage for a hand-picked collection of fans. T-shirts emblazoned with the band's image, tickets for other concerts and CDs were autographed in exchange for gifts from fans under the cameras' watchful eyes. Among the gifts, Robert Trujillo received a traditional Chinese fan.

Metallica took refuge in their rehearsal room. James was smiling and banter was quick, then concentration took over to review a few titles and warm up a little. The band then covered "Breadfan" and revised the arrangements for the song. James tweaked Robert's bass lines and ensured that he was going to play just the right riff... Lars eventually joined them and the band went through the set list, making sure it was balanced throughout the gig. The atmosphere was relaxed, but the band was laser-

focused on the task in hand; they took these new dates in China very seriously.

The lights went down a few minutes later, and the Chinese fans were on fire. Metallica didn't disappoint. The Four Horsemen burst out to deliver a show of classics, with pride of place given to the *Black Album* from which five tracks were played, but they only performed one from *Death Magnetic* that evening. The band treated the Chinese fans to a greatest hits concert for their first date in China. It was a way of making up for lost time and offering early fans a live experience of all the periods that Metallica had gone through while they had been away.

A second show was given the next day at the same venue, then the band pressed on to Korea, Malaysia, Singapore, Indonesia and Brazil before returning to the United States in September for a well-earned break.

Above: James and Kirk playing their first-ever concert in China at the Mercedes-Benz Arena in Shanghai.
Opposite: The four members of Metallica pose at the Toronto International Film Festival in September 2013.

Hit the Lights
For Whom the Bell Tolls
Fuel
Harvester of Sorrow
Welcome Home (Sanitarium)
Broken, Beat & Scarred
The Memory Remains
Wherever I May Roam
The Unforgiven
Sad But True
Orion
Fade to Black
Blackened
Nothing Else Matters
Enter Sandman
Breadfan
Motorbreath
Seek and Destroy

RECORD BREAKERS AT THE CARLINI ANTARCTIC BASE

King George Island, Argentina
8 December 2013

2013 was typical of this period – it was the symbol of the unstoppable performing machine that Metallica had been for several years. They were now the only band to have played on every continent in a single year. The achievement was made official by Guinness World Records at the very end of 2013 when the band gave a concert at the Carlini scientific base, in Antarctica.

The station was established in 1953 and is home to teams of scientists who carry out research on polar and marine environments. Even though they have had a cinema there since 1982 to entertain the teams, Metallica's visit was an exceptional event! The audience was a mix of scientists working on the base, and competition-winners from Latin America.

December is summer in Antarctica. The landscape is bare with no snow, and the band had the stage installed under a transparent dome which let in the icy light of the polar sun. As the performance was taking place in a preserved environment, Metallica had installed solar panels to power the concert's electronics and keep its noise pollution as low as possible so as not to disturb the wildlife that lives on the peninsula.

The area is protected against human intervention. It is home to numerous bird colonies, including more than 14,000 couples of Adélie penguins! For the first time ever, the band had all the spectators wear headsets that broadcast the live concert. Wearing a hat (Lars), a chapka (James) and protective sunglasses, the musicians set out to meet the joyful crowd which was already chanting the band's name. 'Are you ready to make history?' asked James.

The atmosphere at the concert was extremely laid-back, because there were very few spectators. The band also wanted to prove it could still captivate even a small audience. The fans were just a few feet away from the musicians, who performed on a simple stage. The audience sang along with every chorus and every legendary guitar lead, and it almost felt like the band had opened up its rehearsal to the public. They were delighted to be so close to their fans in this special place, far away from the huge stadiums and gigantic world-tour installations. At the end of 2013, all the items on their bucket list had been ticked off.

GLASTALLICA AT GLASTONBURY FESTIVAL
Pilton, England · 28 June 2014

This unprecedented performance in Antarctica was not the end of the promotion for the latest album. It was just a milestone on the journey for Metallica, who pushed on throughout 2014, first in South America (with eight dates in Colombia, Ecuador, Peru, Brazil, Paraguay, Chile and Argentina) before returning to Europe for some major festivals in May. The trip took Metallica to the Sonisphere stages in Finland, then to Norway and Germany, before a stop at the legendary Glastonbury Festival in England on 28 June.

This ode to global pop culture attracted no fewer than 86 different bands and artists, and three huge headliners: Arcade Fire, Kasabian and… Metallica. With the festival's immense popularity and its heavyweight bill, every single ticket sold out within 90 minutes!

When the lights of the main stage at Glastonbury threw their blinding beam onto the sea of people gathered for this unmissable performance, night had already fallen. A forest of flags and banners of all kinds stood tall, dotted around the audience. The stage was a geometric dome,

and a huge flash of light preceded an almost warlike message plastered across a giant video screen at the back of the stage: 'ARE YOU READY FOR GLASTALLICA?'. It was a blue version of the *Ride the Lightning* visual.

"Creeping Death" started with a bang, and the audience went wild. A group of fans had gathered along the entire length of the stage behind the band to get the best view and these lucky few got to experience a perfect show featuring a timeless set list, the band's trademark for festivals and mainstream events. This feast of greatest hits was a success right from the first song, and the Four Horsemen had the audience eating out of their hands.

With 12 tracks and two encores, Metallica entered the Glastonbury history books by becoming the first metal band to headline the iconic festival.

On the strength of this success, the band spent most of 2015 appearing at American and European festivals: Rock in Rio (Nevada), Rock im Revier (Germany), Rockavaria (Germany), Sonisphere (Italy), X Games (Texas), Lollapalooza (Illinois), Reading (England). The band played 16 gigs that year at events they hand picked between February and September. The series of shows marked the end of the long *Death Magnetic* era before the release of a new album, which was planned for the following year.

At the Glastonbury Festival on 28 June 2014,
a mass of fans flock to the stage.

TO INFINITY AND BEYOND...

In 2016 came a follow-up to *Death Magnetic*. *Hardwired... to Self-Destruct* was recorded and written between tours from 2014 to 2016 and released on 18 November. Twelve clips were posted online, one for each track. The album's promotional tour was billed as WorldWired and took Metallica to five continents for 159 concerts spread over three years and six months...

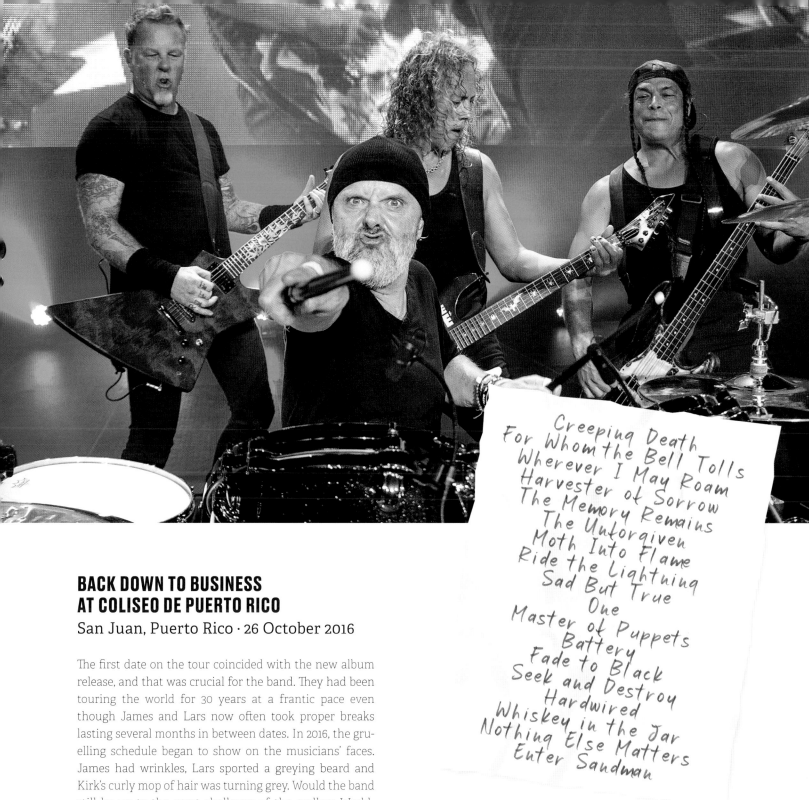

BACK DOWN TO BUSINESS AT COLISEO DE PUERTO RICO

San Juan, Puerto Rico · 26 October 2016

The first date on the tour coincided with the new album release, and that was crucial for the band. They had been touring the world for 30 years at a frantic pace even though James and Lars now often took proper breaks lasting several months in between dates. In 2016, the gruelling schedule began to show on the musicians' faces. James had wrinkles, Lars sported a greying beard and Kirk's curly mop of hair was turning grey. Would the band still be up to the great challenge of the endless World-Wired Tour that lay ahead? Whatever the future held, on 26 October, the arena in San Juan was packed (perhaps more than for the other dates) and the band was laser-focused during rehearsals backstage.

A few minutes before the show, the band members walked along the basement corridor to the stage. James was smiling and high-fiving the crew, wishing them all the best for the gig. But did a band as experienced as Metallica still need luck? The band answered the question with its first thumping track. As soon as his thrash riff got going, the fierce grin on James's face showed he was ready for a fight. Meanwhile, Lars was headbanging like a wild teenager.

Creeping Death
For Whom the Bell Tolls
Wherever I May Roam
Harvester of Sorrow
The Memory Remains
The Unforgiven
Moth Into Flame
Ride the Lightning
Sad But True
One
Master of Puppets
Battery
Fade to Black
Seek and Destroy
Hardwired
Whiskey in the Jar
Nothing Else Matters
Enter Sandman

A colourful concert! Each light effect is timed to the music to the thousandth of a second.

Kirk and Lars went for an understated look (had there been any wardrobe changes since the *Black Album* tour?), while James seemed to have plunged back into the thrash uniform of the band's heyday: tight black jeans, boots, and sleeveless leather vests with patches on the back. You'd think he was about to go on a road trip with the Hells Angels from Vegas!

The show was spectacularly staged. The light and pyrotechnical effects were timed to the nearest thousandth of a second, matching the music perfectly. The icing on the cake was that the band had installed three giant screens, two on the sides of the stage and one behind the musicians. It was an enormous investment, but the spend was worthwhile when Metallica banged out 18 tracks with the precision of skilled snipers. Most of the hits they played on that evening were from legendary albums before *St. Anger*. Unlike the concerts that were supposed to promote the new album, Metallica started the tour with a set of greatest hits and only two new tracks from *Hardwired... to Self-Destruct*.

The day after the premiere, the band flew to Ecuador, then Colombia, Guatemala and Costa Rica, before heading over to Europe for a few promotional shows. There were a handful more dates when the band got back to the States in December, before they headed to Asia on 11 January for a five-date tour.

Hardwired... to Self-Destruct:
the latest addition

In line with *Death Magnetic*, Metallica's tenth album honoured its roots. It begins with a barrage of artillery: machine-gun-style snare drum, Barbarossa guitars and an ultra-precise kick. *Hardwired... to Self-Destruct* also has an incredibly effective first single (aptly named "Hardwired")! Produced and mixed by Greg Fieldman, the two-record album released on 18 November 2016 contains 12 tracks. It shot to the number one sales spot in the United States, with nearly 291,000 copies sold in one week.

Fact: this is the first studio album that the band produced themselves on their Blackened label. With a more precise sound than its predecessor, *Hardwired... to Self-Destruct* is one of the rare recent Metallica records of which several tracks are regularly played on stage, such as the intro to the first single and its satisfying warlike rolls.

Hardwired
Atlas, Rise!
For Whom the Bell Toll
Creeping Death
The Unforgiven
Now That We're Dead
Moth Into Flame
Wherever I May Roam
Confusion
Halo On Fire
Sad But True
One
Master of Puppets
Fade to Black
Seek and Destroy
Battery
Nothing Else Matters
Enter Sandman

ASIAWORLD-EXPO
Chep Lap Kok, Hong Kong
20 January 2017

On 20 January, the band played its very first gig in Hong Kong, an area with a long-standing Westernized culture but which still had extremely strong influences from the Chinese regime. The fans here had never seen their favourite band and the atmosphere was electric. As soon as the doors opened, the audience raced down the aisles screaming, desperate to get the best spots in the mosh pit. The Hong Kong fans were ready: Metallica flags, promo T-shirts and horns-up hand gestures abounded.

This was a single-date show, and Metallica reshuffled their set list to include many more new tracks from the last album. Six tracks from *Hardwired... to Self-Destruct* were played that evening, just one from *Kill'Em All*, three from *Ride the Lightning*, one from *...And Justice for All* and two from *Master of Puppets*. Five songs from the *Black Album* also made the cut. The audience went into a trance from the first bars of "Hardwired", and the screams persisted for the duration of the gig. When James asked the crowd: 'Do you want heavy? Metallica gives you heavy babyyy!' the crowd went wild, and the band launched into a molten steel version of "Sad But True".

James, Kirk, Lars and Robert play their first concert in Hong Kong on 20 January 2017.

LIGHT EFFECTS AT THE NEW COLISEUM
Uniondale, New York · 17 May 2017

After their trip to Asia, the band had a few gigs in Denmark in February, then on 12 May embarked on a new marathon tour, exploring every corner of the American continent, including Mexico, Brazil, Argentina and Chile. In all, they played six gigs in South America up until April, when the band returned to the United States for 75 shows in the biggest leg of the gigantic tour. They began in Maryland, then travelled to Pennsylvania, New Jersey, New York, Massachusetts, Ohio, Missouri, Colorado, Iowa, Texas, Illinois and Florida.

On 17 May the Metallica machine arrived at the New Coliseum in Uniondale, New York. Just like before each performance on this tour, when Ennio Morricone's introduction resonated around the room, everyone backstage was deep in concentration. A few seconds before walking to the stage, the musicians formed a circle, holding each other by the shoulders. James led the pre-show pep talk: 'Is everybody ready? Yeah? Let's go and let's kick some asses! Let's enjoy it, do what we've got to do! OK let's kick asses! Woooo!' The musicians then crossed the room, cutting through the crowd between two steel barriers, battered with flashes and telephone lights.

The stage was in the centre of the arena, overlooked by a video screen with images flashing up to the jerky rhythm of the snare drum bursts during the intro to "Hardwired" which ran in a loop. It was fair to say the band had retained its 'wow' factor.

When the band stepped onto the stage, thousands of dots lit up under their feet, creating a futuristic atmosphere that matched perfectly with the artwork on the cover of their latest album. Metallica was all about showmanship and everything was put together with surgical precision, no detail left to chance, from the choreographed entry on stage to the slightest meticulously crafted transition. The brutal savagery of the early days had been overtaken by professionalism. But the armoured offensive at the top of the show was proof that violence and a yearning for thrash were still part of the band's identity, as shown by the decidedly effective "Hardwired"!

The American tour went on until August. From 2 September, Metallica returned to Europe for two months and played 15 shows in Denmark, the Netherlands, Germany, England, Scotland and Belgium. They also gave another series of gigs in France between 8 and 12 September, because the French fans couldn't get enough.

James and Kirk put on a carefully choreographed show in Uniondale. The band serves up a real spectacle.

Hardwired
Atlas, Rise!
For Whom the Bell Tolls
Ride the Lightning
The Unforgiven
Now That We're Dead
Moth Into Flame
Harvester of Sorrow
Welcome Home (Sanitarium)
The Four Horsemen
Sad But True
One
Master of Puppets
Fade to Black
Seek and Destroy
Blackened
Nothing Else Matters
Enter Sandman

FRENCH KISS: HALLE TONY GARNIER
Lyon, France · 12 September 2017

This iconic venue in the city of Lyon hosted Metallica for the second time in its history. The first gig was played here on 23 May 2010. When the band arrived in this 19th-century building with its industrial metallic architecture, they struggled to build their usual staging. Pulleys, hoists, trusses and immense metal structures were installed and suspended by steel cables from the venue's beams. The idea was to transform the cavernous hall into a structure that could accommodate the band's lighting, the majority of which needed to be installed above the stage. On this occasion, the band had suspended light cubes from the ceiling around the square stage, making the set-up look like an MMA ring, and the musicians prowled like gladiators surrounded by a furious audience.

This was the only show aside from the two in Paris, and the Halle was packed to capacity, with an electric atmosphere. Professional to the end, the band performed a set that highlighted the new album (six tracks) and the hits from the *Black Album* (four tracks). It set tracks from *St. Anger* and *Death Magnetic* aside, as had been the norm for several months. When the time came for the last song ("Enter Sandman"), pyrotechnic effects and leaden riffs left the Lyon fans in ecstasy, as they belted out the backing vocals in unison on all the choruses. 'Lyon, did you have fun tonight?', asked James, smack bang in the middle of the break, before picking back up and finishing the anthology track at the end of the set.

With the glaring house lights up, the musicians ended the concert by saying warm goodbyes to the audience, who gave them a standing ovation, bare arms in the air.

In total, the WorldWired tour included 68 concerts in Europe and continued until August 2019, when Metallica flew to the United States for a new anniversary project.

Despite the passing years, James and the audience appear more connected than ever.

S&M2 AT THE CHASE CENTER
San Francisco, California
6 and 8 September 2019

The project to celebrate the *S&M* album's 20th anniversary saw the light in the spring of 2019. The band wanted to repeat the experience with the San Francisco Symphony, this time conducted by Edwin Outwater and Michael Tilson Thomas to replace the late Michael Kamen. The idea was that during the two days of recording and concerts, the tracks on *S&M* would be embellished with arrangements by Michael Kamen, and new pieces added with symphonic parts composed by Bruce Coughlin. Unlike during the first edition of S&M, the members of Metallica appeared very comfortable on stage, having 20 years of touring under their belts. On the 1999 version, the band tended to fade behind the plethora of classical musicians and the aura of 'classical music'. Now the musicians stood centre stage on a set whose design was reminiscent of their regular tours. The orchestra was arranged in a circle around the band with the conductor, Bruce Coughlin, facing his alter ego Lars Ulrich, who beat time for Metallica. Another notable difference was that while the staging for S&M left little room for light effects, times had changed in 2019. The band had installed several huge cylindrical video screens above the stage, which projected their images. The audience stood around the band and everyone had a great view. And what a performance! As well as the magic that the symphony orchestra had already brought to S&M, this time the band brought its confident power and experience. More mature, more precise, fully assuming their roles as musicians, the members of Metallica delivered an impressive performance that lasted more than two and a half hours!

Previous page: Robert Trujillo and Kirk Hammett during a concert in Cologne (Germany), 13 June 2019.
Left: Lars and Kirk during the new edition of the famous S&M concert, which was performed on a central, circular, rotating stage.

The year 2019 ended on a sour note for the band, which they blamed on the temporary departure of James Hetfield for rehab to treat his alcohol addiction. The final Australian leg of the WorldWired Tour was postponed for the same reason. In 2020, the Coronavirus pandemic impacted the band hard, and during the following months they only played filmed concerts that fans could watch online. Metallica did not get back on stage until 16 September 2021 in San Francisco, in good old California, where they began almost forty years earlier.

THE RETURN OF THE DIRTY KIDS

During a daunting post-Covid comeback, Metallica continued their journey in Europe then played a series of concerts in the United States in the autumn of 2022. The tour ended on 16 December with the very last show in their hometown, Los Angeles. In 2023, a new chapter opened for the Four Horsemen as they worked on the release of a brand-new album: *72 Seasons*. The tour that went with it took a new format in which the band expressed their urge for freedom. They had absolutely nothing to prove.

PARIS IS BURNING
Paris, France · 17 and 19 May 2023

For this new promotional tour, Metallica were determined to treat their audience to a unique experience to make up for the Covid years, which brought many cancelled gigs and had clearly disappointed fans. This new adventure planned to take in no fewer than 22 cities, throughout Europe, Canada and Mexico. It kicked off in Amsterdam on 27 April 2023. It was a simple concept, yet the fans were desperate to see it. As well as their revamped staging (the famous Snake Pit was centred to the stage for the occasion), the band planned to give two shows in each city and follow the slogan: 'No Repeat Weekend'. Each of the two gigs had a different set list, a concept that allowed the organizers to set up double ticketing system, so fans could see both shows, or the one they preferred. Metallica lifted highlights from its entire back catalogue to create two different gigs. Needless to say, fans were delighted and tickets sold out fast. At the Stade de France on 17 May, Metallica played their 25th concert in the French capital. The stadium was at boiling point, a sea of bodies had filled the arena, in which huge pylons had been erected to support the giant cylindrical screens for the live broadcast. This new set-up positioned the band right in the middle of its screaming fans. For only the second time in their history, Metallica decided to open the first Parisian show with "For Whom the Bell Tolls", followed by a thunderous "Ride the Lightning". The fans couldn't get enough as they sang in spine-tingling unison. Firmly in their groove, the Four Horsemen pushed on with "Holier Than Thou" before launching into the French premiere of "Lux Aeterna" from their latest album. The mammoth audience was dazzled by a slew of greatest hits: "Fade to Black", "Nothing Else Matters", "Sad But True", "Blackened", before an anthology finale with "Seek & Destroy" and "Master of Puppets". Then came the 48-hour interval. Two days later, the lucky few who were able to afford tickets for both events were back at the stadium. It was 19 May and "Creeping Death" rumbled around the enormous concrete venue. Just like in the previous show, the set list gave pride of place to the band's hits ("Harvester of Sorrow", "The Unforgiven", "Battery"), but one of the standout moments was a version of "One", which was introduced by a spectacle of flames and fireworks.

Opposite: Lars Ulrich and Robert Trujillo in their element on stage at the Johan Cruyff Arena, Amsterdam, 29 April 2023.
Right: James Hetfield kicks off the tour in Amsterdam on 27 April 2023.

DOWNLOAD FESTIVAL
Castle Donington, England
8 and 10 June 2023

As is often the case with Metallica, a tour in Europe meant a chance to reconnect with old friends and perform again on familiar stages. These two concerts in the United Kingdom were the perfect example, with the band playing at the Download Festival in Castle Donington. The double date falls outside the strict framework of the M72 World Tour, but follows the same framework: two new concerts with two different set lists. Even though the band preferred not to use its current tour staging for the festival, the main stage at Download was fitted with an apron. But that did not rule out an abundance of light effects (and pyrotechnics during the introduction to "One"). Wartime

photographs were also projected onto the two screens near the stage. As for every date on this tour, the band loved meeting their fans. They seemed liberated to be playing their greatest hits in front of an audience of dedicated followers, who erupted in rapturous applause as soon as the first notes of each familiar track rang out. It was almost a jubilee for Metallica in this green and pleasant land. The band gave two concerts as a kind of tribute to its own music, in two greatest-hits set lists.

Above: A year earlier, the band had already appeared at the Download Festival in Hockenheimring, Germany, on 24 June 2022.

72 seasons:
wild animals on the prowl

This new record, which springs into boisterous action from the very first notes, was released on 14 April 2023. The album cover featured a child's bedroom. The bed and toys scattered on the floor appeared to have been charred with napalm, leaving no doubt as to the band's artistic choices for this new studio launch. This was an A to Z of old-school thrash. The 12 tracks included all the gimmicks of the genre in songs that ranged from 3 minutes 21 seconds for "Lux Aeterna", one of the most successful tracks, up to the finale "Inamorata", which continues for a whole 11 minutes 10 seconds. Another brainchild of Greg Fidelman, the contemporary, square-on production style of *72 Seasons* perfectly highlights the guitar runs and drum-playing genius provided by Lars, who was more on point than ever when it came to beating out uptempo rhythms. Special mention goes to the mixing on Robert Trujillo's bass, which seems more audible than on some past productions. *72 Seasons* offers up a feast of beautifully concocted tracks that promises to satisfy the appetites of Metallica fans hungry for mosh-pits and headbanging. What more could you want?

SOFI STADIUM
Los Angeles, California
25 and 27 August 2023

After a series of shows in Europe (the Netherlands, France, Germany and Sweden) Metallica returned home for more gigs in Canada and then the United States. Having called at New Jersey, Montreal and Texas, the great global thrash circus rocked up to Los Angeles, California. It was 25 August 2023 and the crowd at SoFi Stadium was buzzing. For the first night's show, Metallica struck fast and hard with the relentless and terrifyingly effective "Creeping Death". It is fair to say that as the musicians had been playing such a wide repertoire on their tour, they had reached an astonishingly high standard of playing. James was at his sharpest and even though his face bore the signs of passing years, his clear voice was more confident than ever. He had lost none of his outstanding right-hand guitar playing, which formed the backbone of the band's music.

Now a full-fledged member of the Metallica family, Robert Trujillo held up the backing vocals and confidently partnered Lars on the rhythm section. While the keenest ear may have noticed some shortcuts on the fastest portions of the tracks, on the drums as well as during Kirk's slightly more cautious guitar solos, the band still had fire in their bellies and the audience was eager for more. The magical atmosphere of "Sad But True" in the hot Californian night was evidence of that. Singing a cappella, James projected the hit's unforgettable lyrics and left the microphone for a moment to allow the audience to sing in his place before letting a silence settle to build up to the smooth chords of the introduction. Metallica knows its fans, and knows how to give them want they want. After this memorable gig, the musicians took the show to Arizona, California, Missouri and Michigan. Showing signs of maturity and (at long last) channelled enthusiasm, the Four Horsemen took a proper break from their M72 World Tour during the winter of 2023 and didn't return to the road until spring the following year.

James Hetfield and Kirk Hammett are back in Los Angeles for a memorable concert on 25 August 2023 at SoFi Stadium.

CONCLUSION

After two years of pandemic-induced cancellations and disappointments, the band picked up its endless journey to stages around the world. In 2021, Metallica had the United States in their sights (Illinois, Kentucky, California, Florida, Georgia, Texas), with 13 dates planned through to December, then a truly packed programme starting in February 2022. In the spring, the band chose to return to the international stage in South America with six dates (Chile, Argentina, Brazil) before heading back over to Europe (Denmark, the Netherlands, Italy, Czech Republic and Germany). The climax of the tour was in Clisson, France, at the gigantic Hellfest: the ultimate event for European metalheads. It was a first for Metallica and the festival went all out to welcome the titans of thrash.

This "edition of the century" – as festival director Ben Barbaud describes it – took place over two consecutive week-

ends, between 17 and 26 June, and brought together 350 bands, including the legendary Guns N'Roses and Scorpions. Metallica was scheduled for the Sunday, the closing night. The musicians delivered a powerful show before an ocean of fans. Bringing its legend to life and realizing that Metallica's presence at the event made it a consecration of sorts, the staff had prepared an impressive stage that included immense video screens, an apron on which the musicians would be able to reach the middle of the crowd, and above all, spectacular pyrotechnic effects.

Calibrated to demonstrate that the band had lost none of its aura during the pandemic, the show-of-force 16-track set list packed in almost all the band's hits ("Creeping Death", "Enter Sandman", "Wherever I May Roam", "Sad

But True", "Nothing Else Matters", "For Whom the Bell Tolls", "Fade to Black", "One" and so on) before ending with a "Master of Puppets" (certainly the most eagerly awaited) anthology. At the end of spring 2022, the track suddenly drew a huge number of new fans because it was featured in the ever-popular Netflix series *Stranger Things*. During the Season 4 finale, one of the characters (who plays a young fan of 80s thrash) plays the track on his guitar in a bid to defeat the evil creature perched on the roof of a motorhome. It's a breathtaking scene and the unstoppable track with condensed metallic power struck a chord with millions of spectators around the world. After 40 years, Metallica has become a symbol of aggressive music from the early 1980s, which now permeates every corner of modern pop culture.

This crowning achievement and recognition would never have happened if Metallica had not fought against all odds and travelled to every corner of the planet.

It would have been easy to give a souless list of all the concerts Metallica have played during their colossal career, we could go into impressive statistics, work out how many people have seen them live, or even cite how many tons of equipment were used for the legendary Hellfest concert.

But, ultimately, none of these figures in isolation could possibly capture the power of the band's onstage performances, and the sacrifices they have made to keep their music alive, to fuel this incredible dream machine. A Metallica gig is about so much more than live music and stage performances. The band strive to pursue their journey, tirelessly treading the paths they have already travelled a thousand times. Their goal is to cultivate their legacy and nourish the bond they have with their audience. With each gig, James, Lars, Kirk, Robert and their fans celebrate the idea that they are tied together by something bigger than the sum of their parts. And nobody wants to let that go. This form of almost magical mysticism, which seems to draw strength from an inexhaustible source of energy, is what characterizes the founding legends of our culture. Seeing Metallica in concert is the celebration of a 40-year-old legend, a story that began in the suburbs of the southern United States.

PHOTOGRAPHY CREDITS

BIBLIOGRAPHY

Metallica: Justice for All Joel McIver, Omnibus Press, 2005.
Metallica, Enter Night, Mick Wall, Camion Blanc, 2012.
Metallica, The four horsemen du heavy metal, Martin Popoff, Le Chêne-E/P/A, 2016.
www.metallica.com.

ACKNOWLEDGEMENTS

I would like to thank everyone at EPA, Camille Dejardin whose patience and constant listening ear created just the right conditions for me to work on this book; Julien Henry for this new collaboration on a theme – music – which is dear to both of us; Antoine Béon at Hachette Heroes without whom this formidable team would not have come together to create this wonderful project; Sébastien Gicquel – a fan of Metallica before the Eternal – with whom I spoke about the concerts given by legendary members of the band; and of course my family, who had to listen/watch/endure live shows by Metallica for long hours over the last 12 months.

Translated from French by Ruth Simpson.

First published in Great Britain in 2024 by

Greenfinch
An imprint of Quercus Editions Ltd
Carmelite House
50 Victoria Embankment
London EC4Y 0DZ

An Hachette UK company

A CIP catalogue record for this book is available
from the British Library

HB ISBN 978-1-52943-827-7
Ebook ISBN 978-1-52943-828-4

10 9 8 7 6 5 4 3 2 1